EXTENSITY

A COLORING BOOK

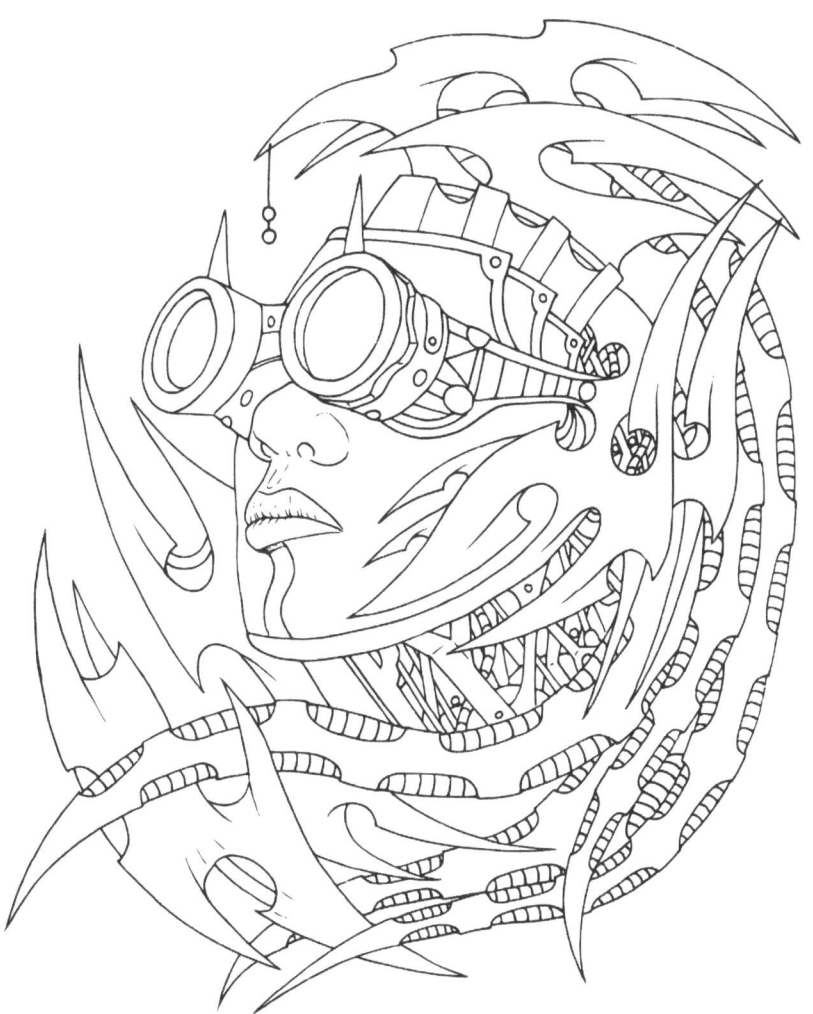

ARTWORK BY REX FINDLEY

EXTENSITY

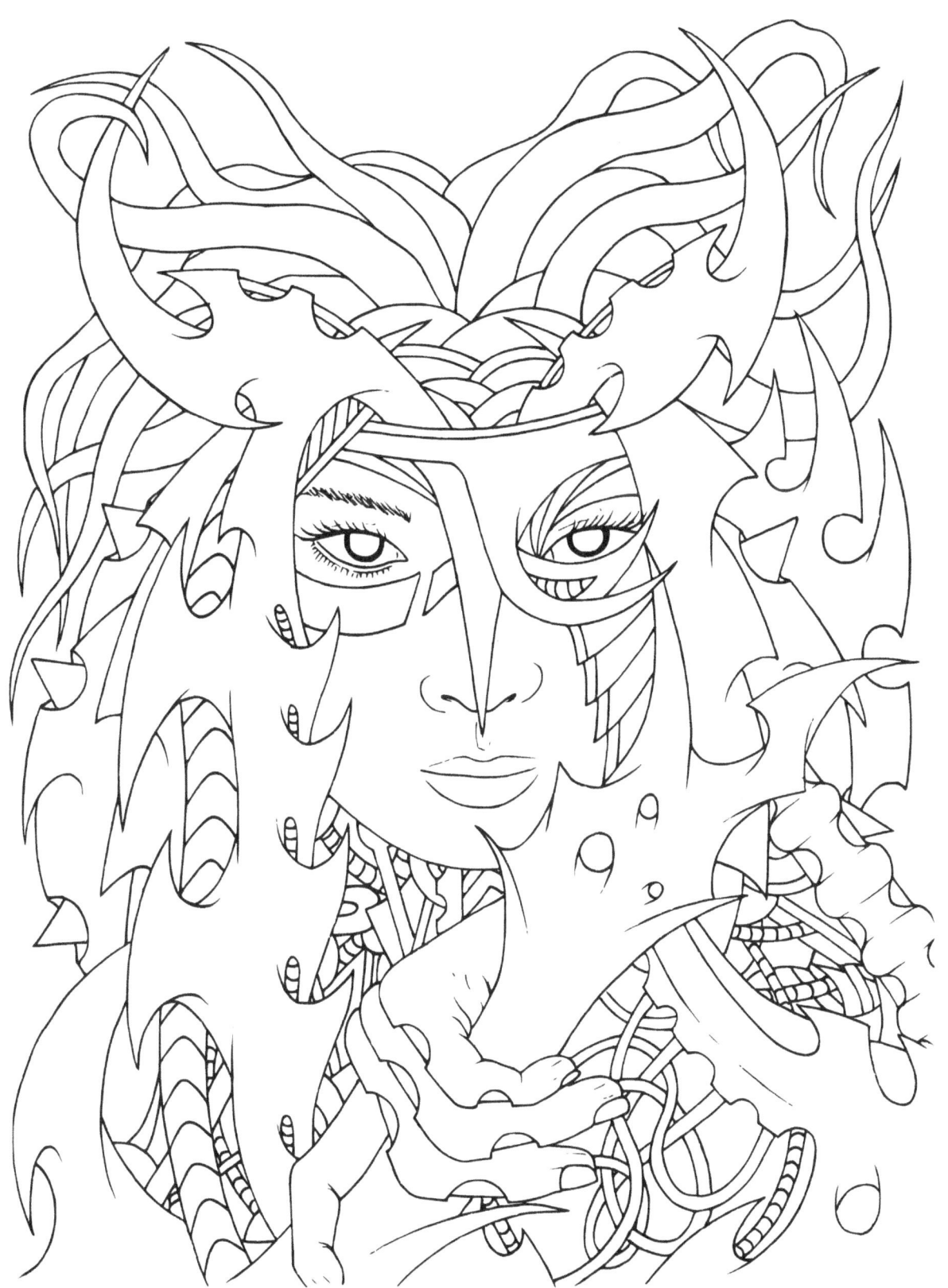

EXTENSITY

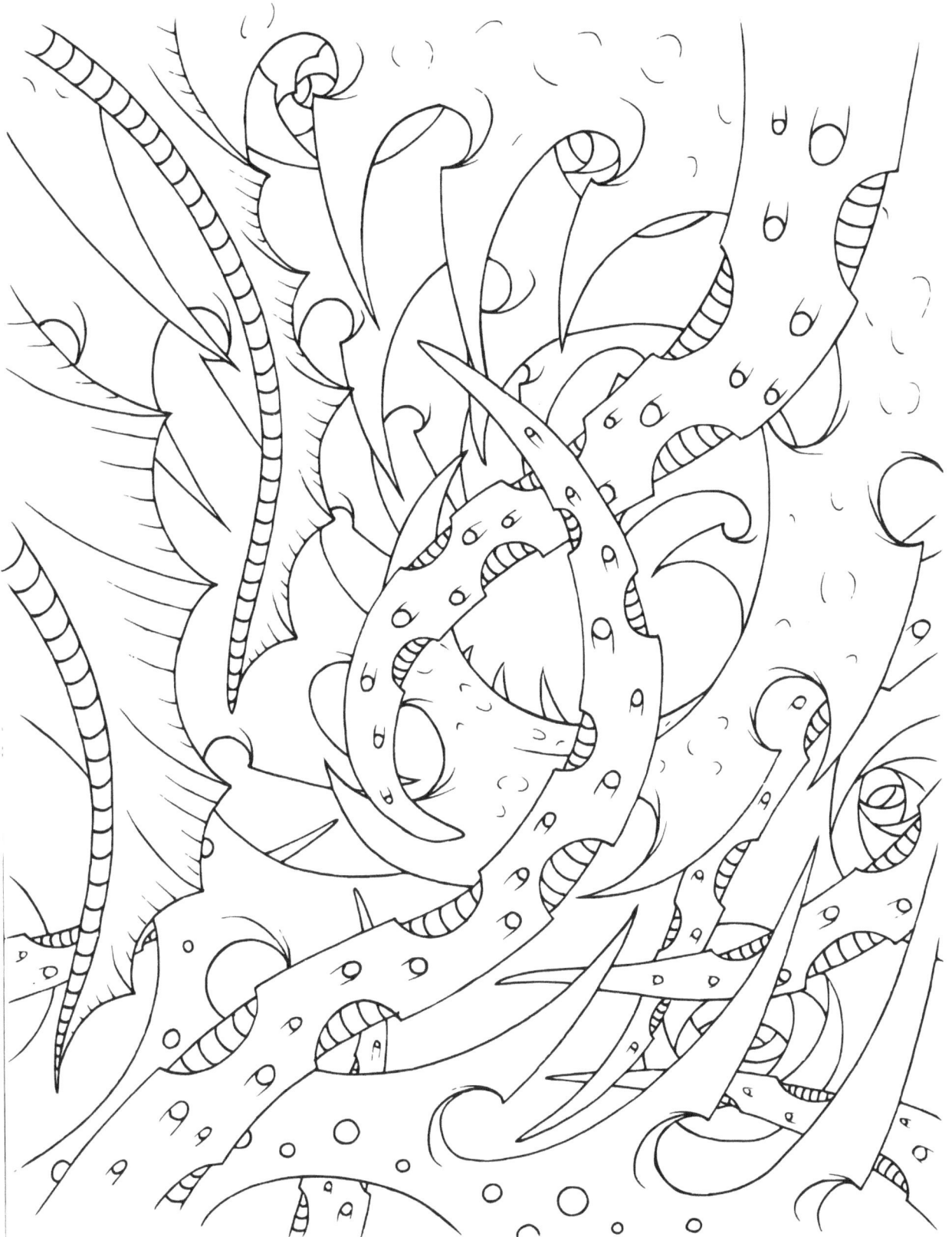

EXTENSITY

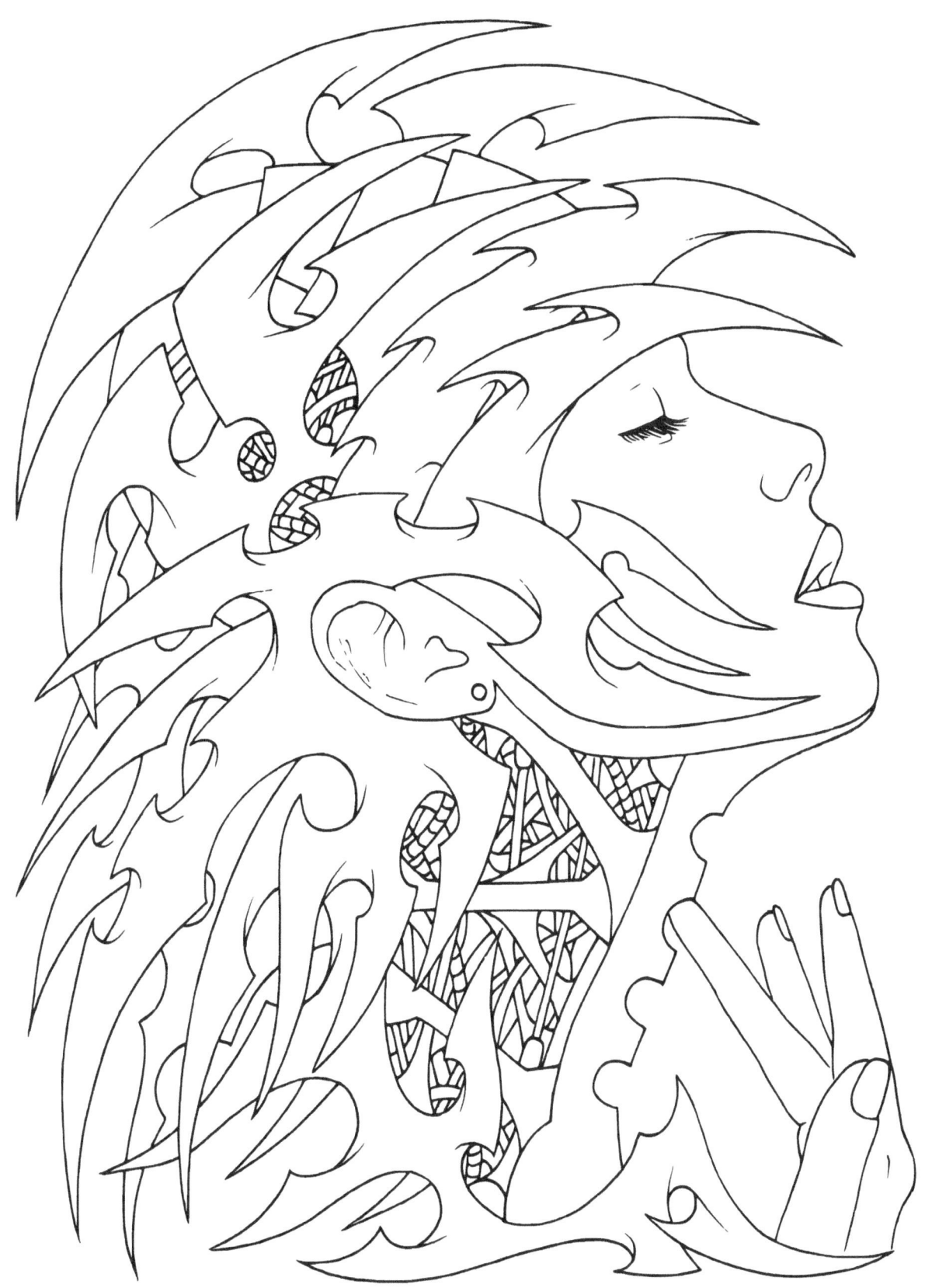

EXTENSITY

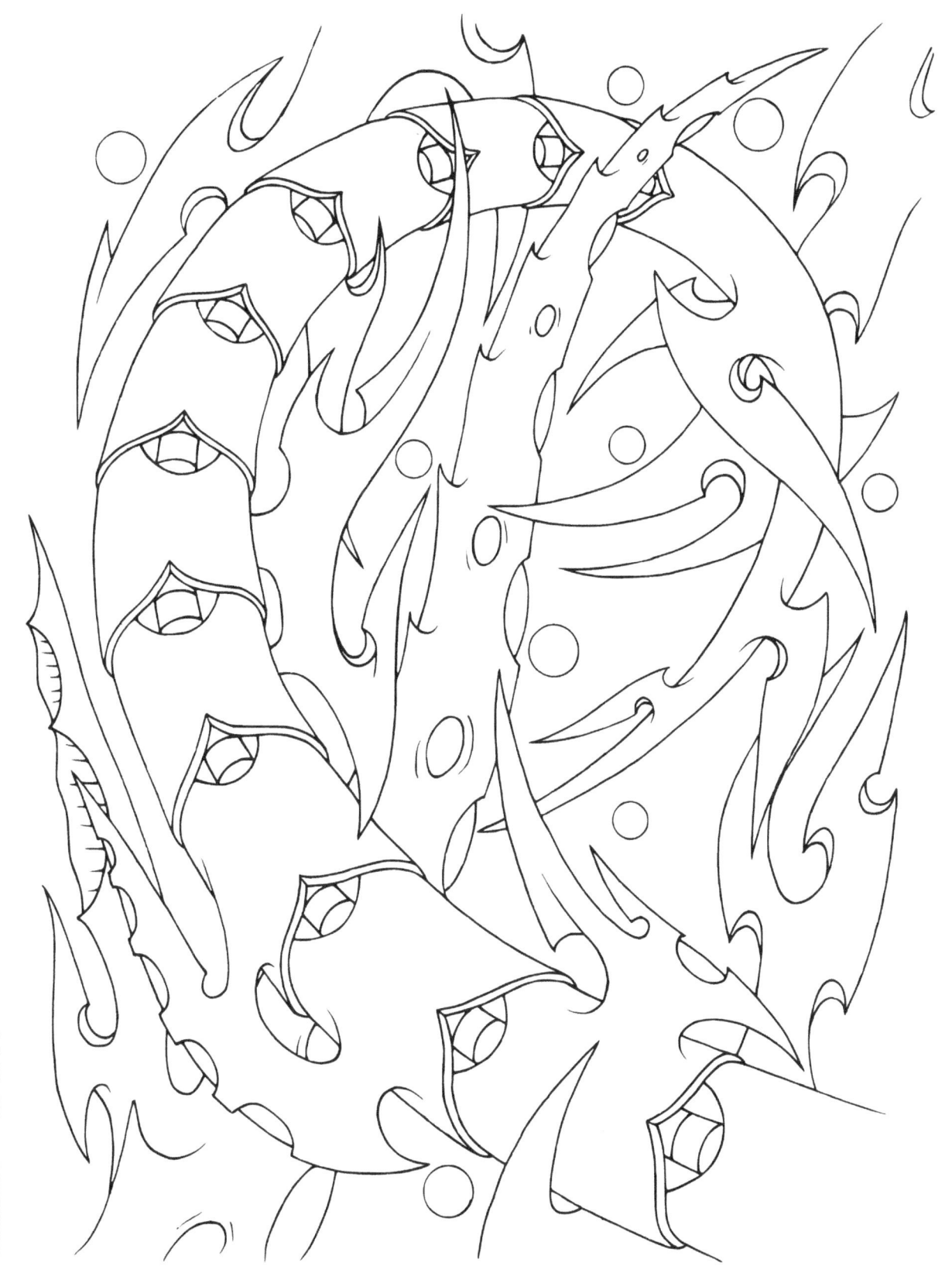

EXTENSITY

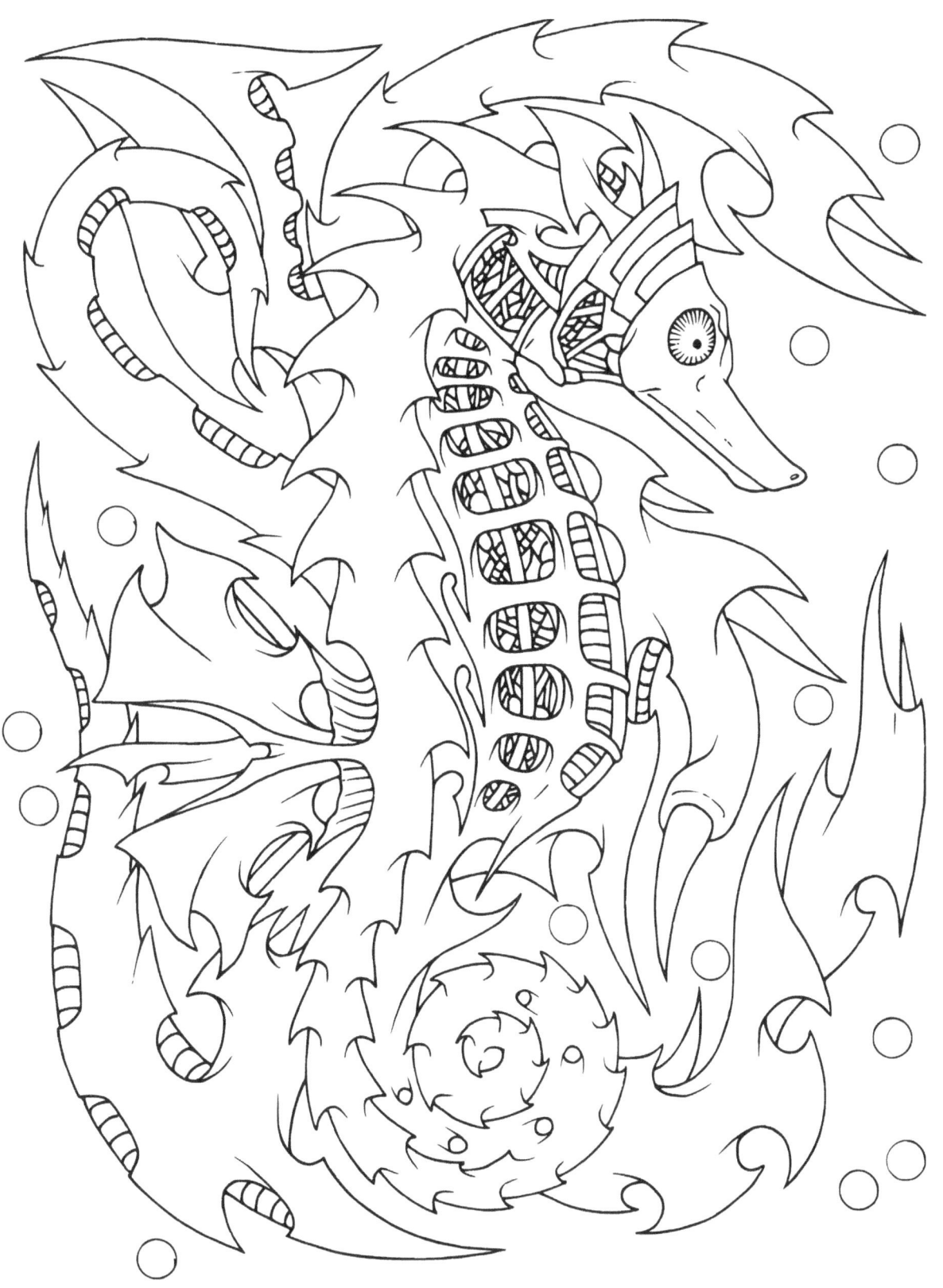

EXTENSITY

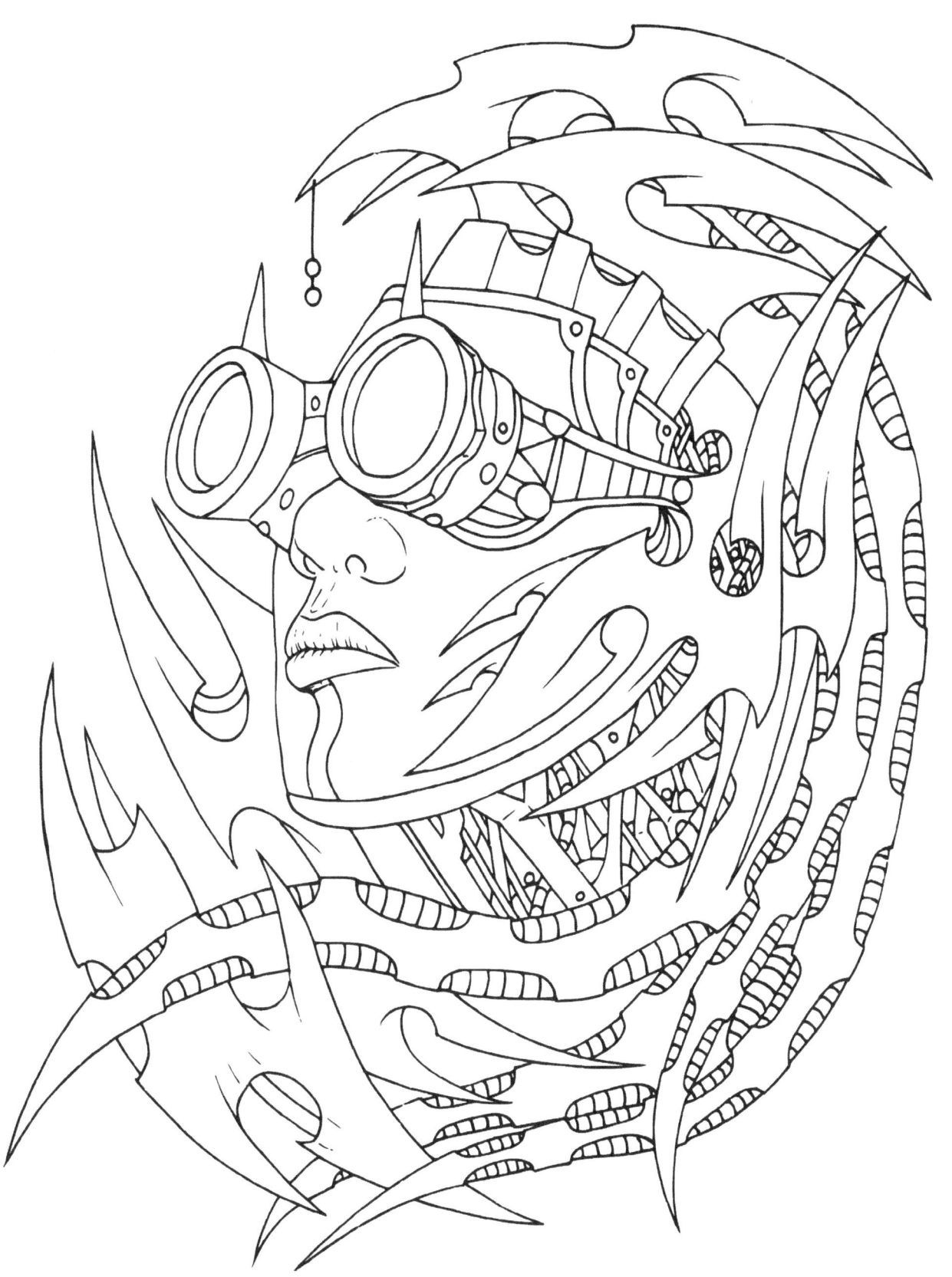

EXTENSITY

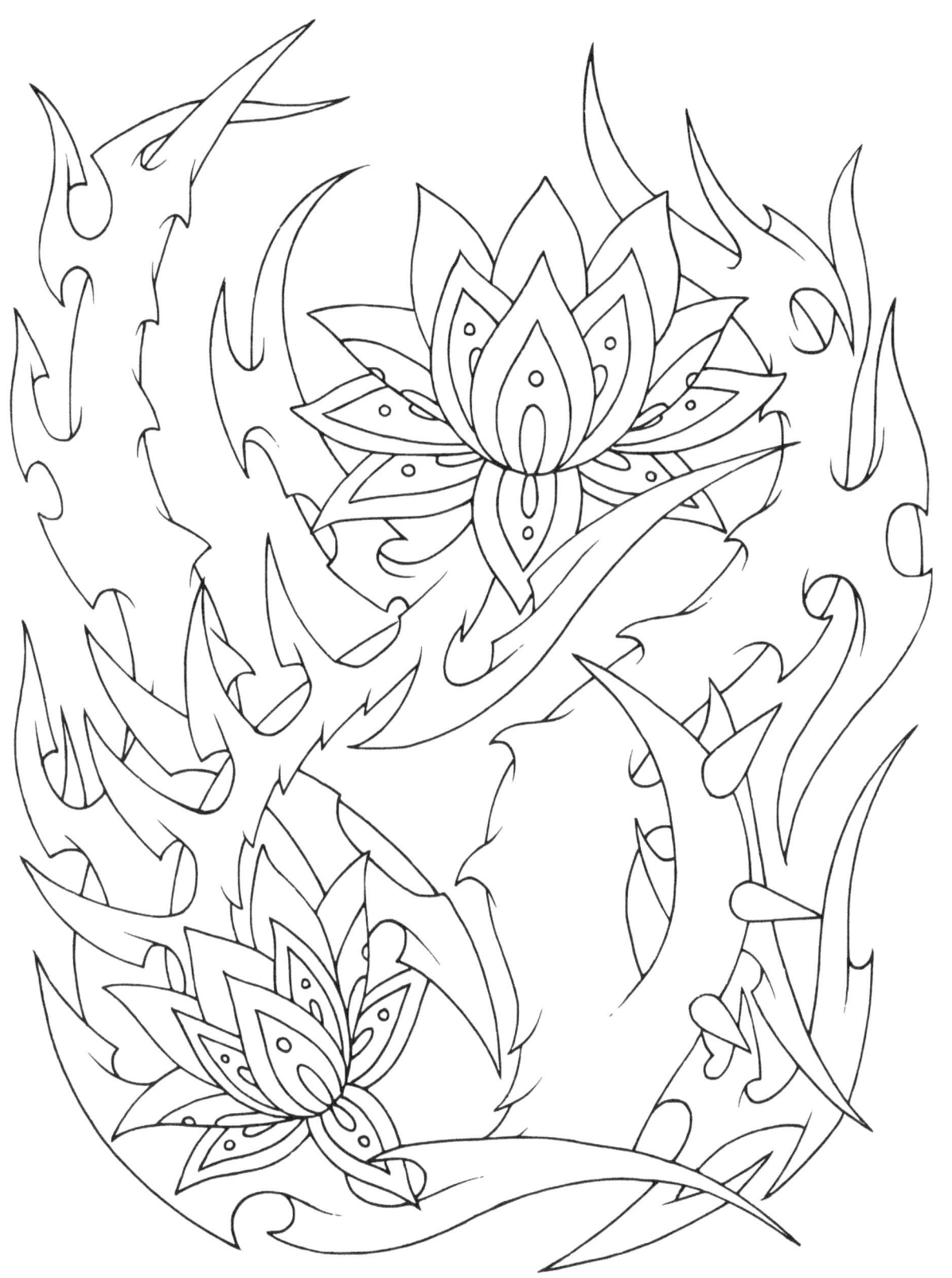

EXTENSITY

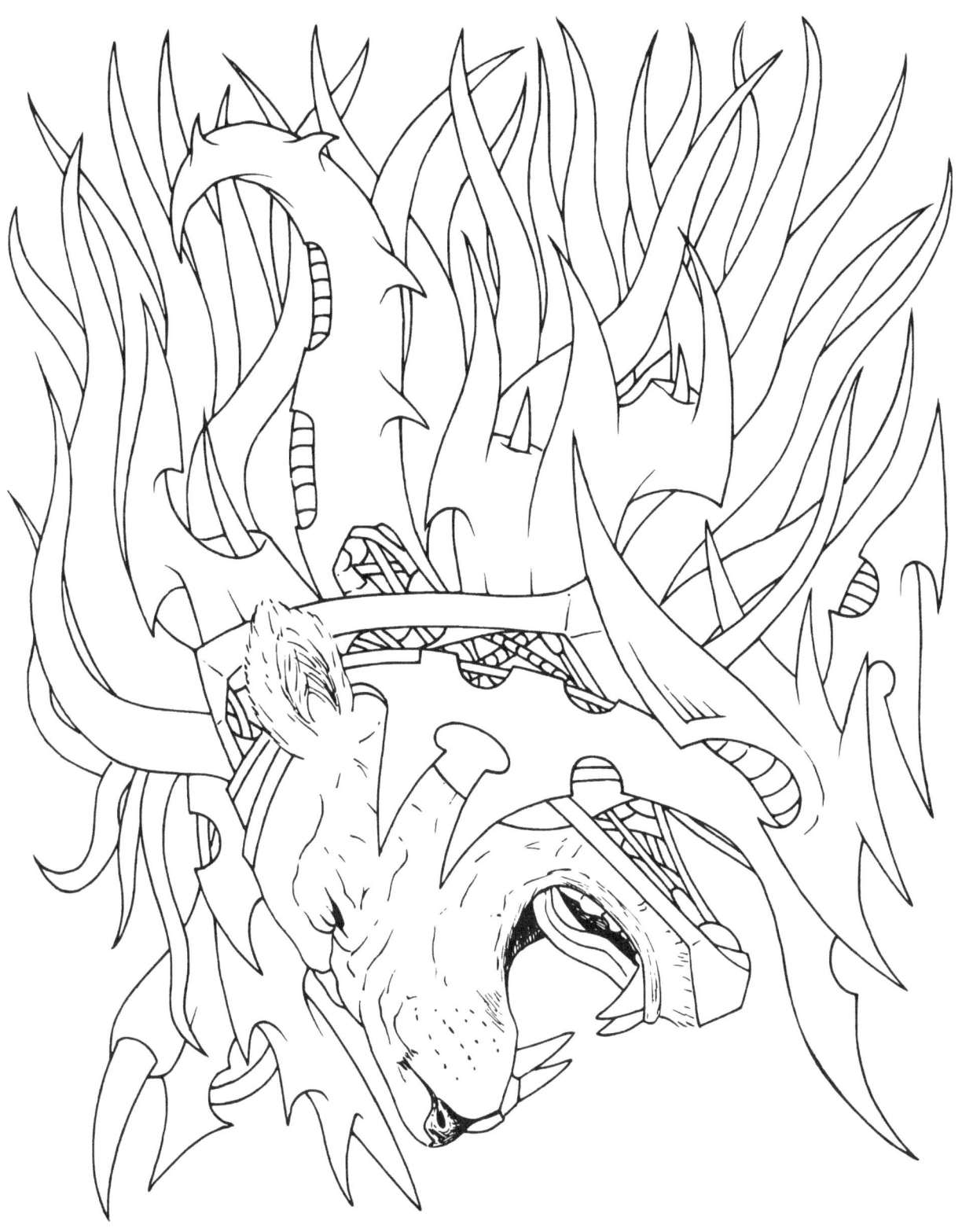

EXTENSITY

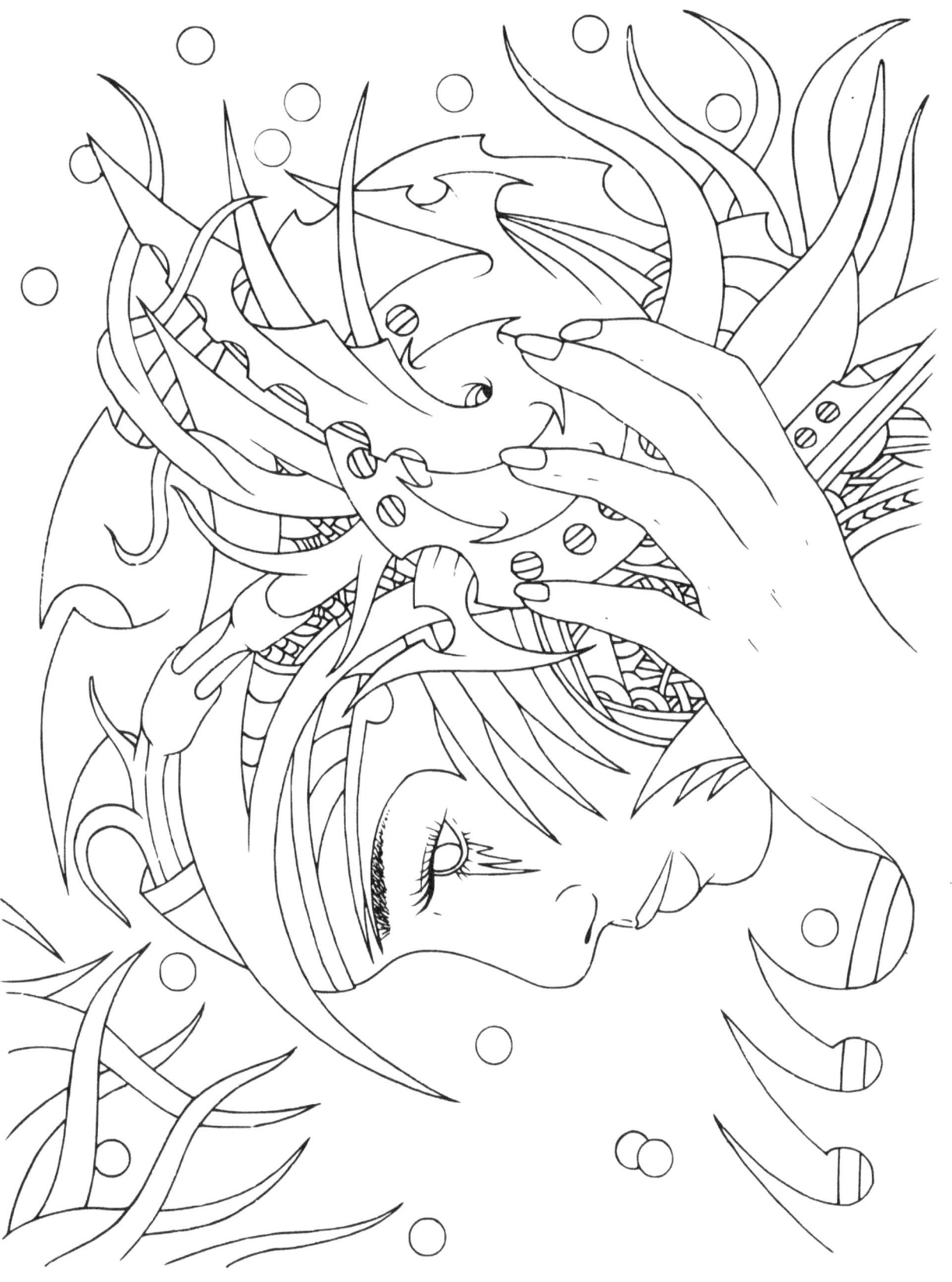

EXTENSITY

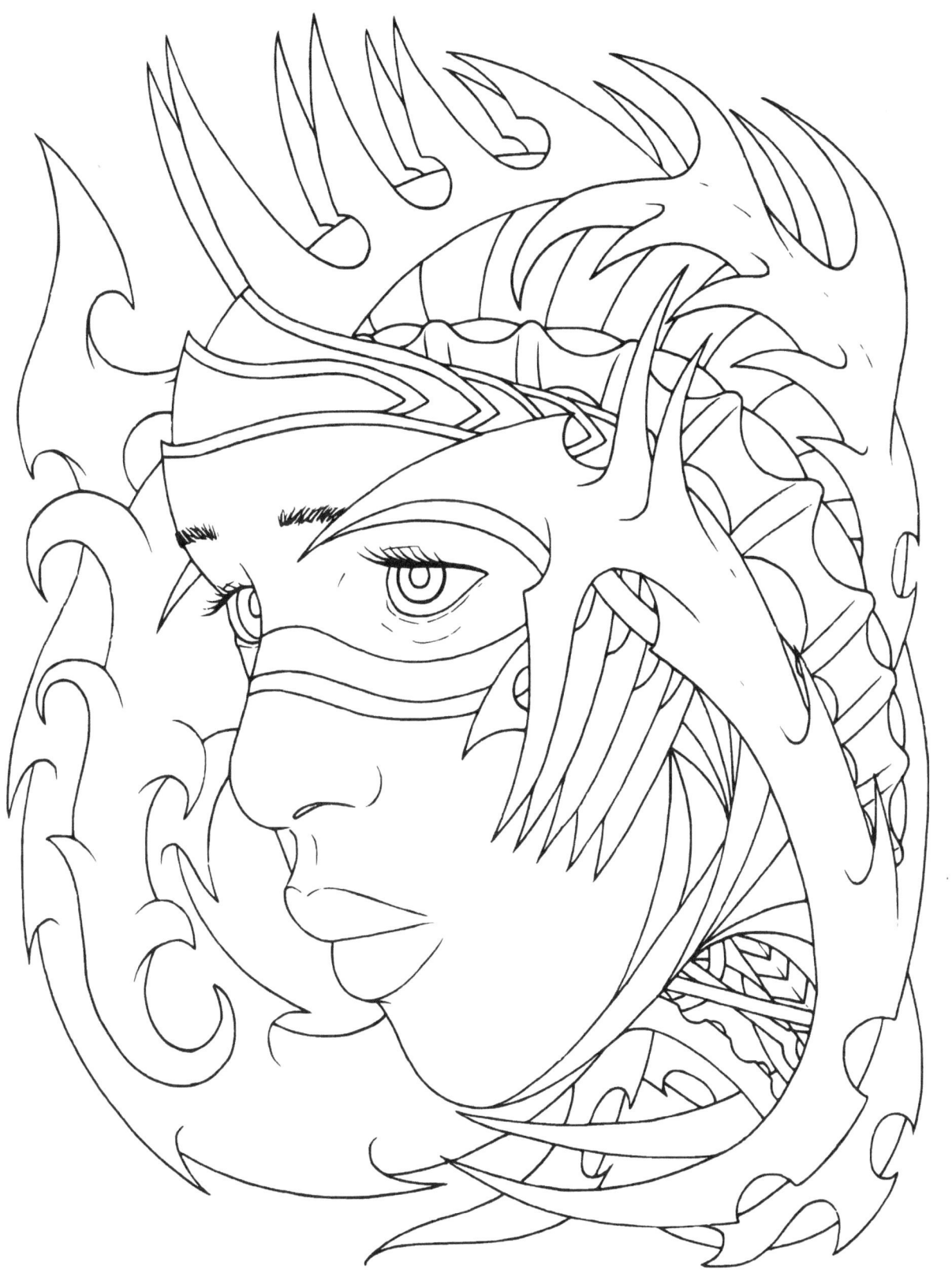

EXTENSITY

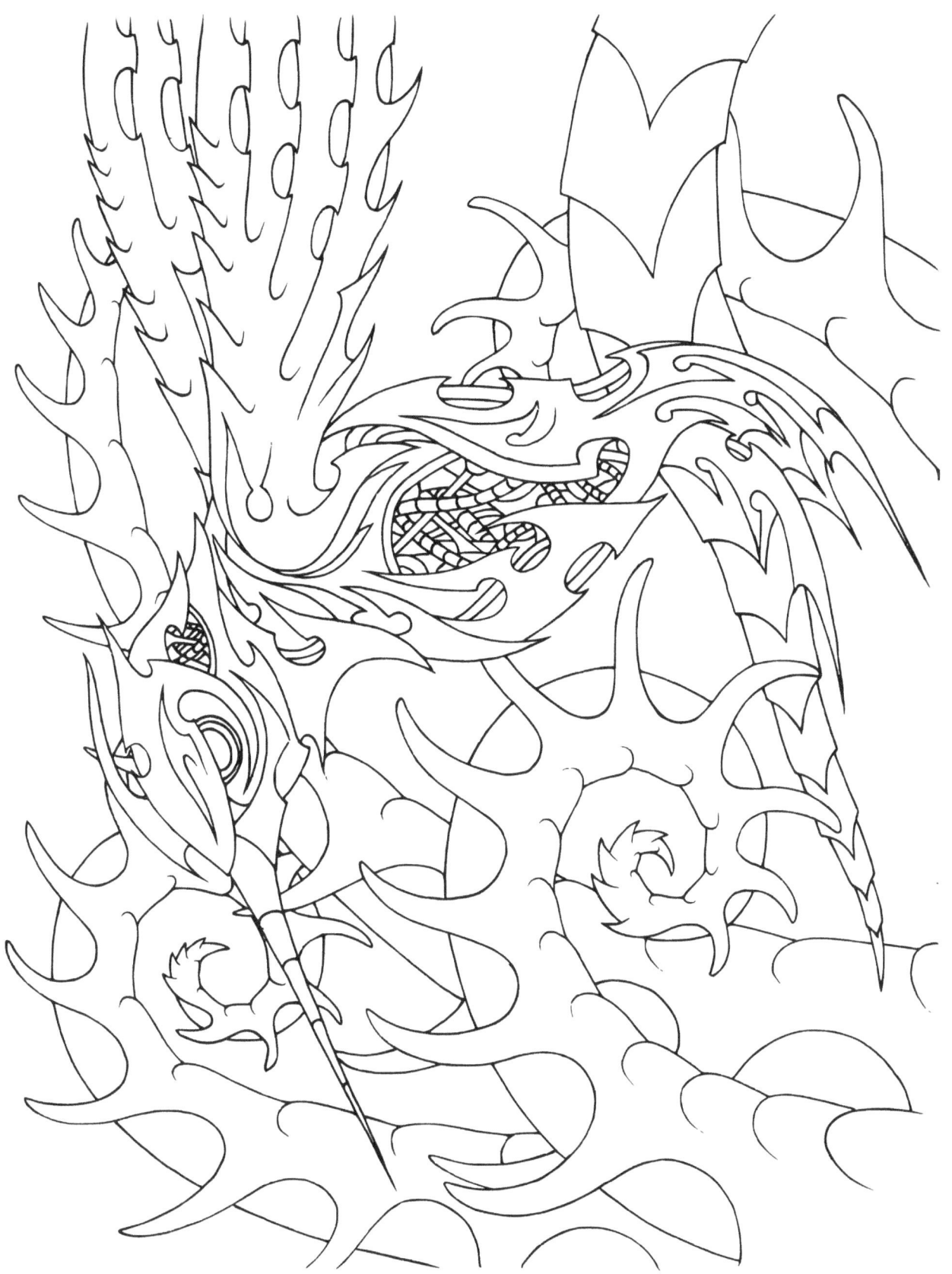

EXTENSITY

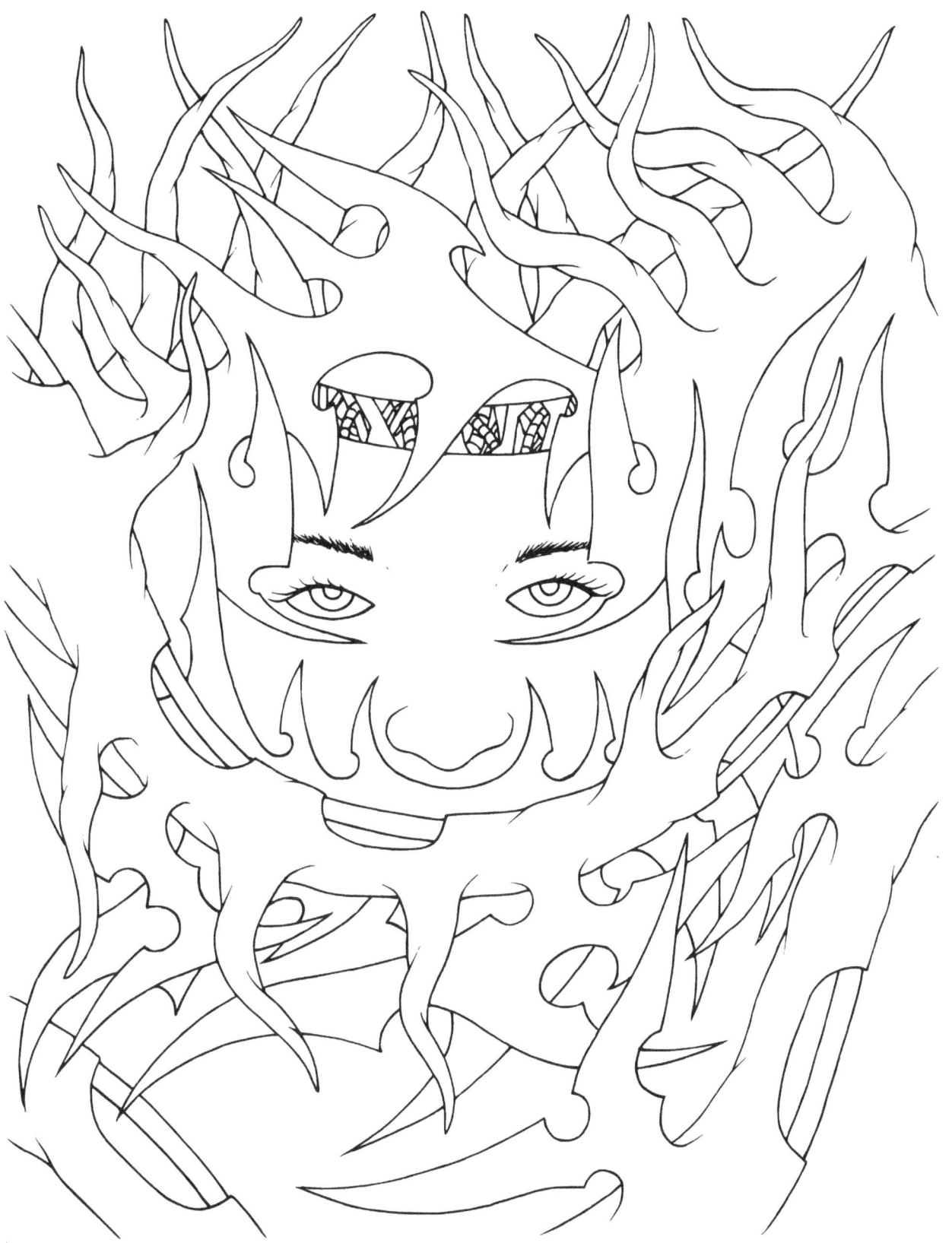

EXTENSITY

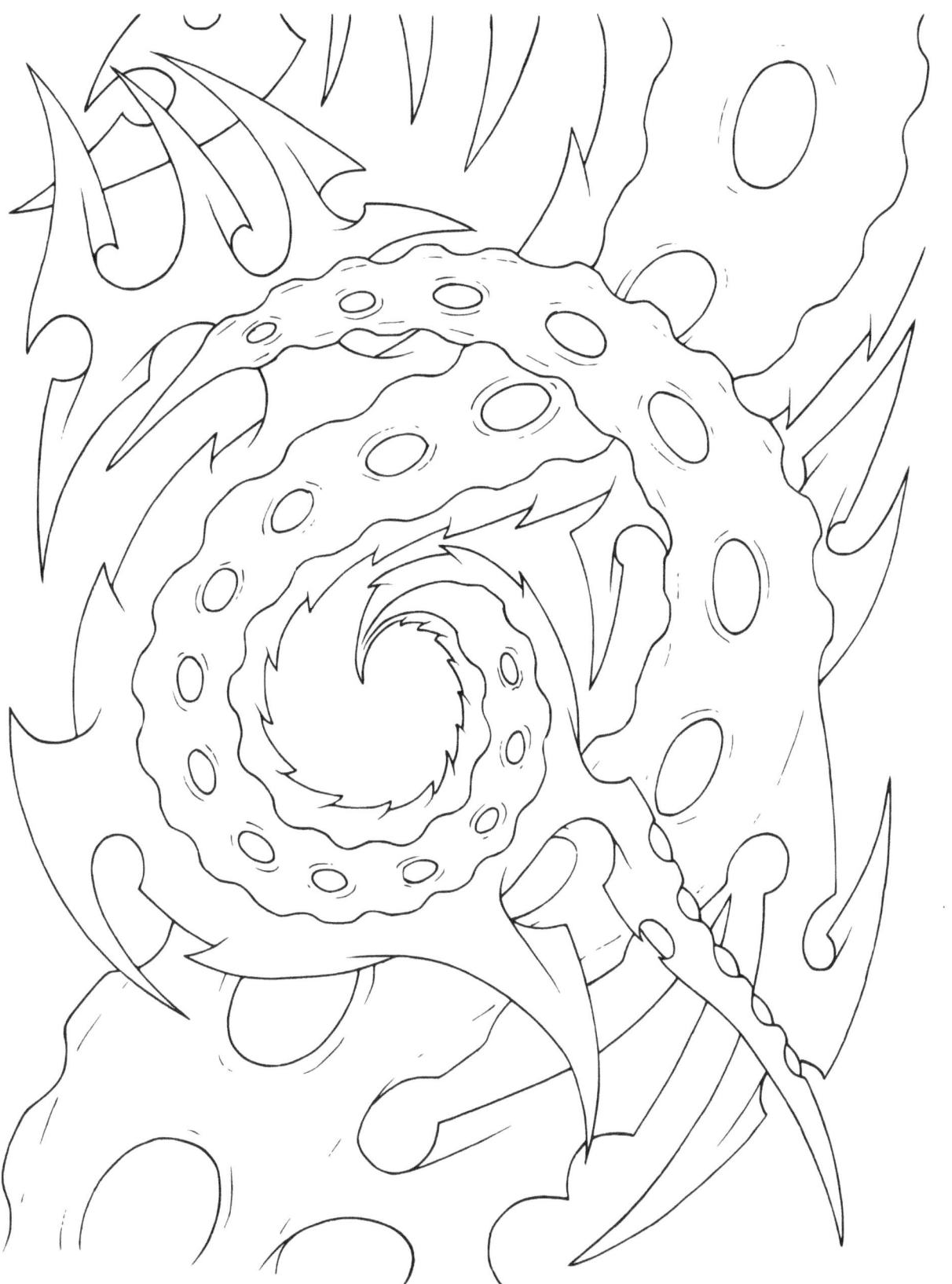

EXTENSITY

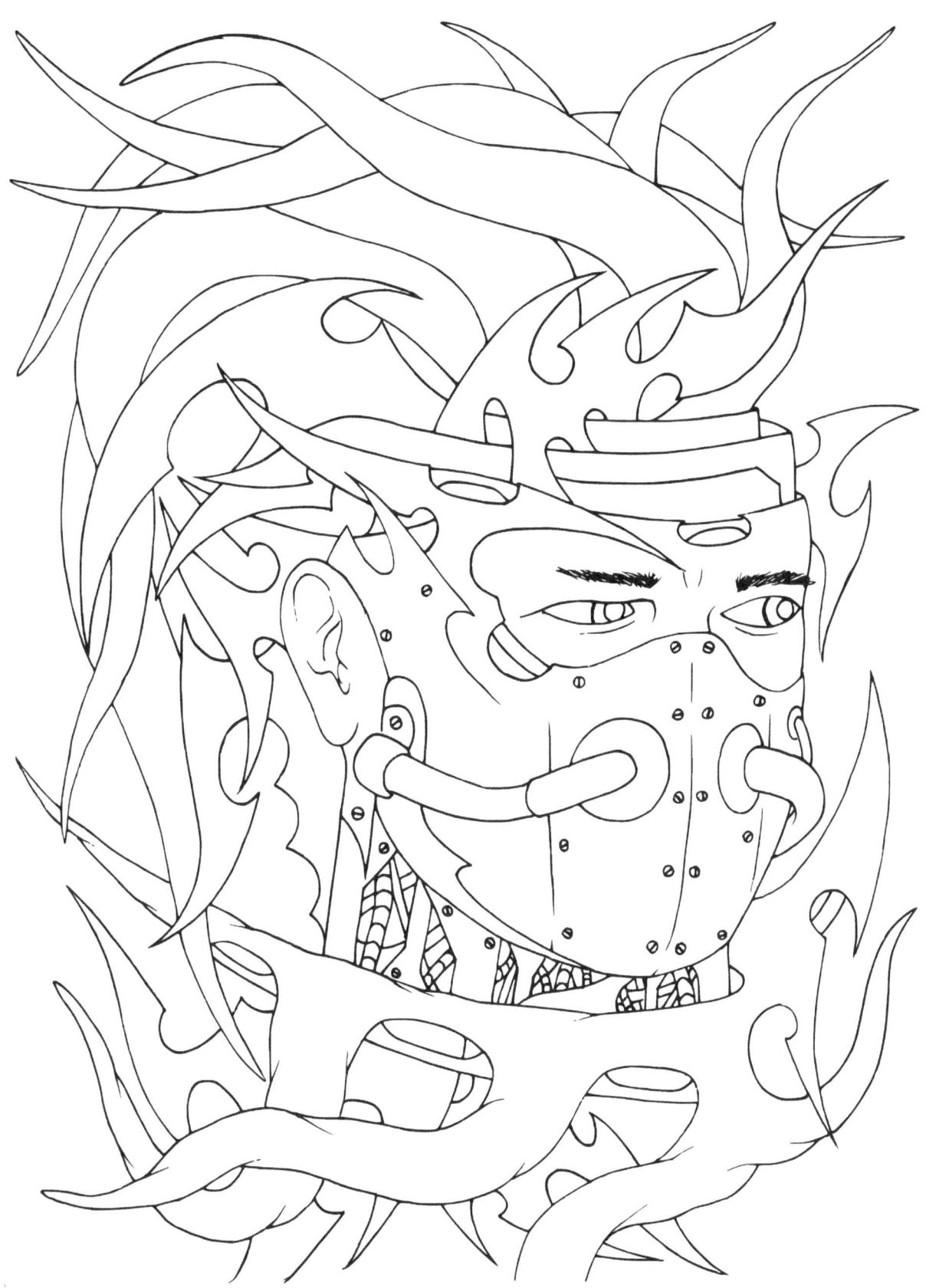

EXTENSITY

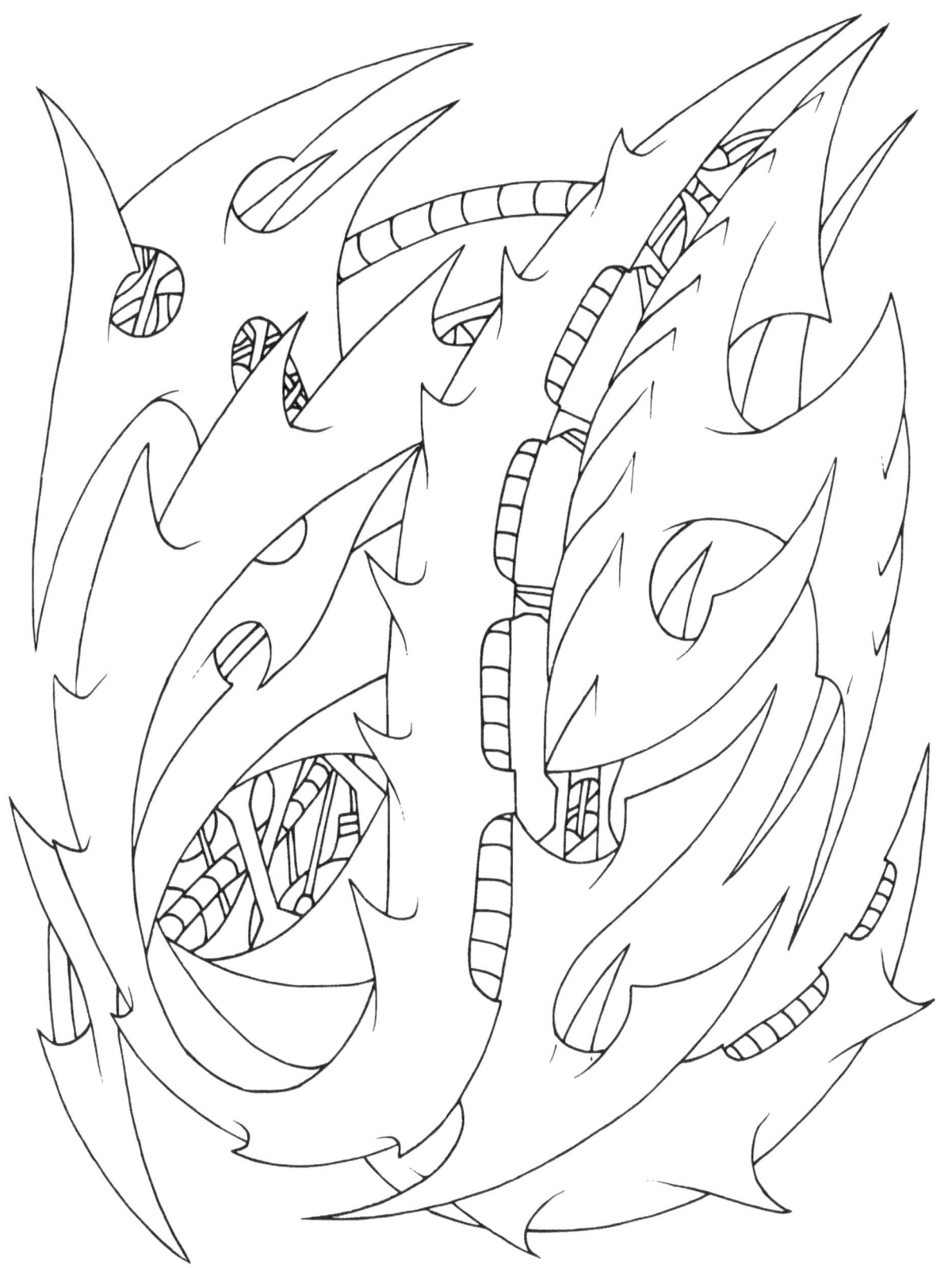

EXTENSITY

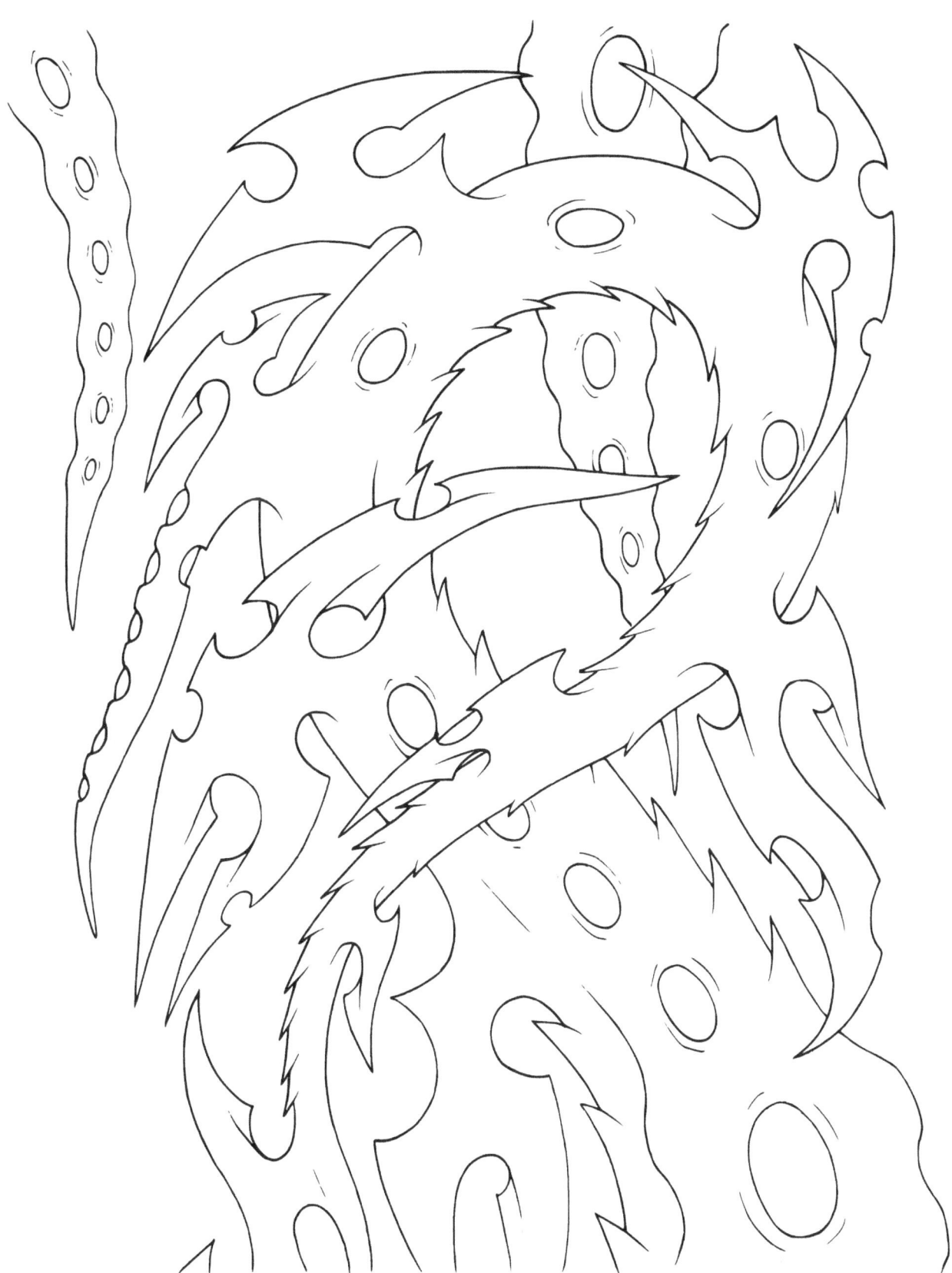

EXTENSITY

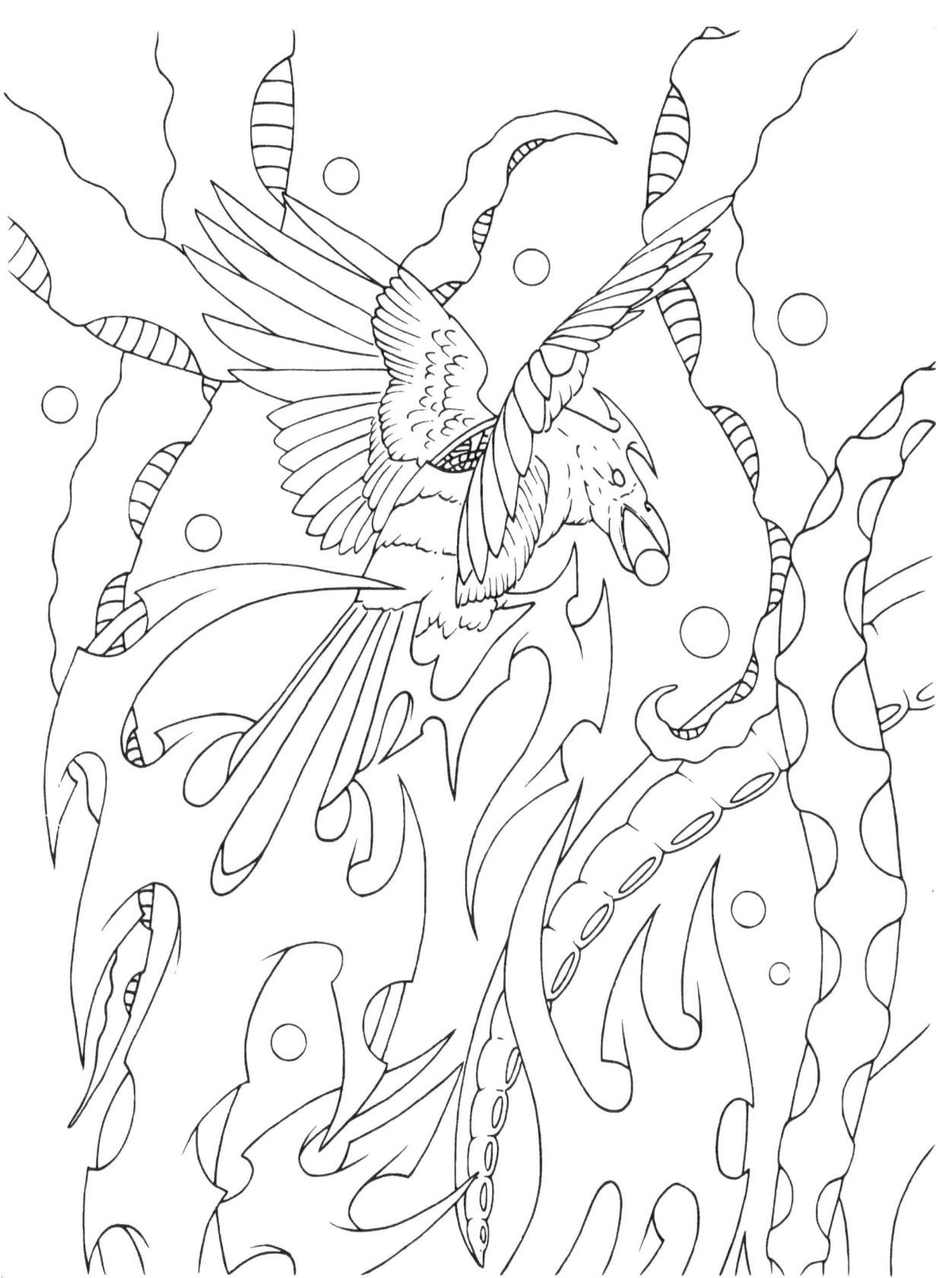

EXTENSITY

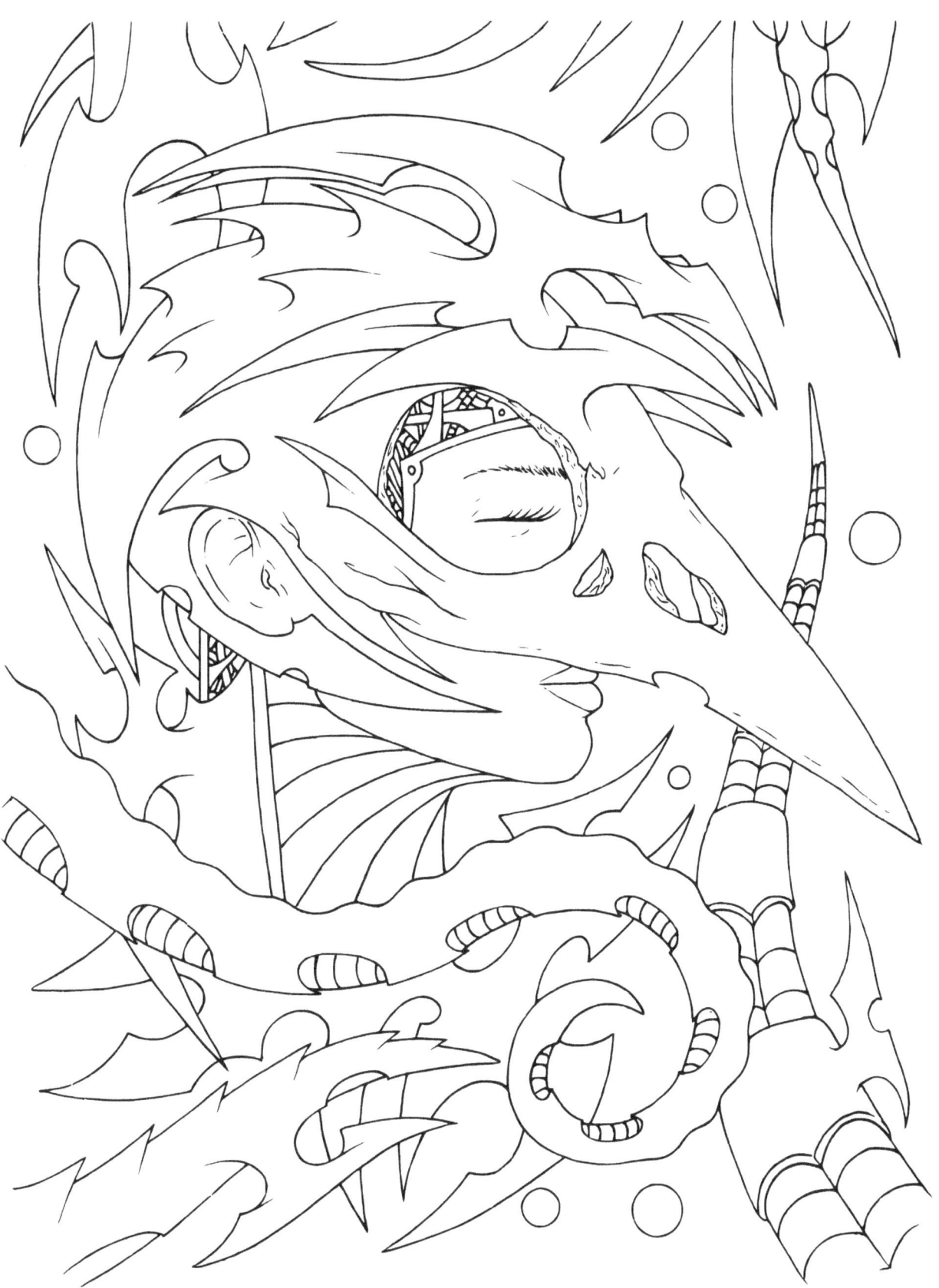

EXTENSITY

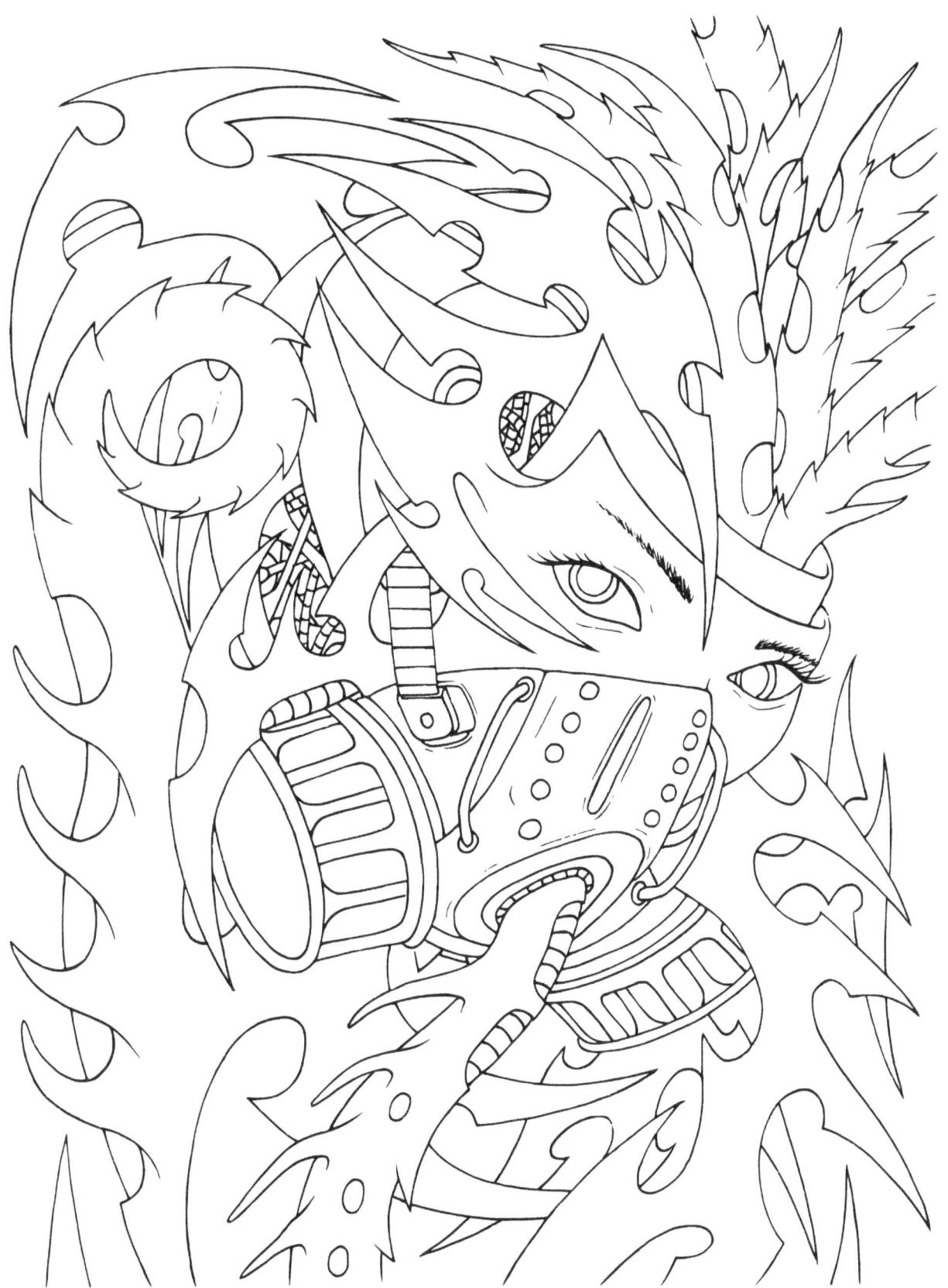

EXTENSITY

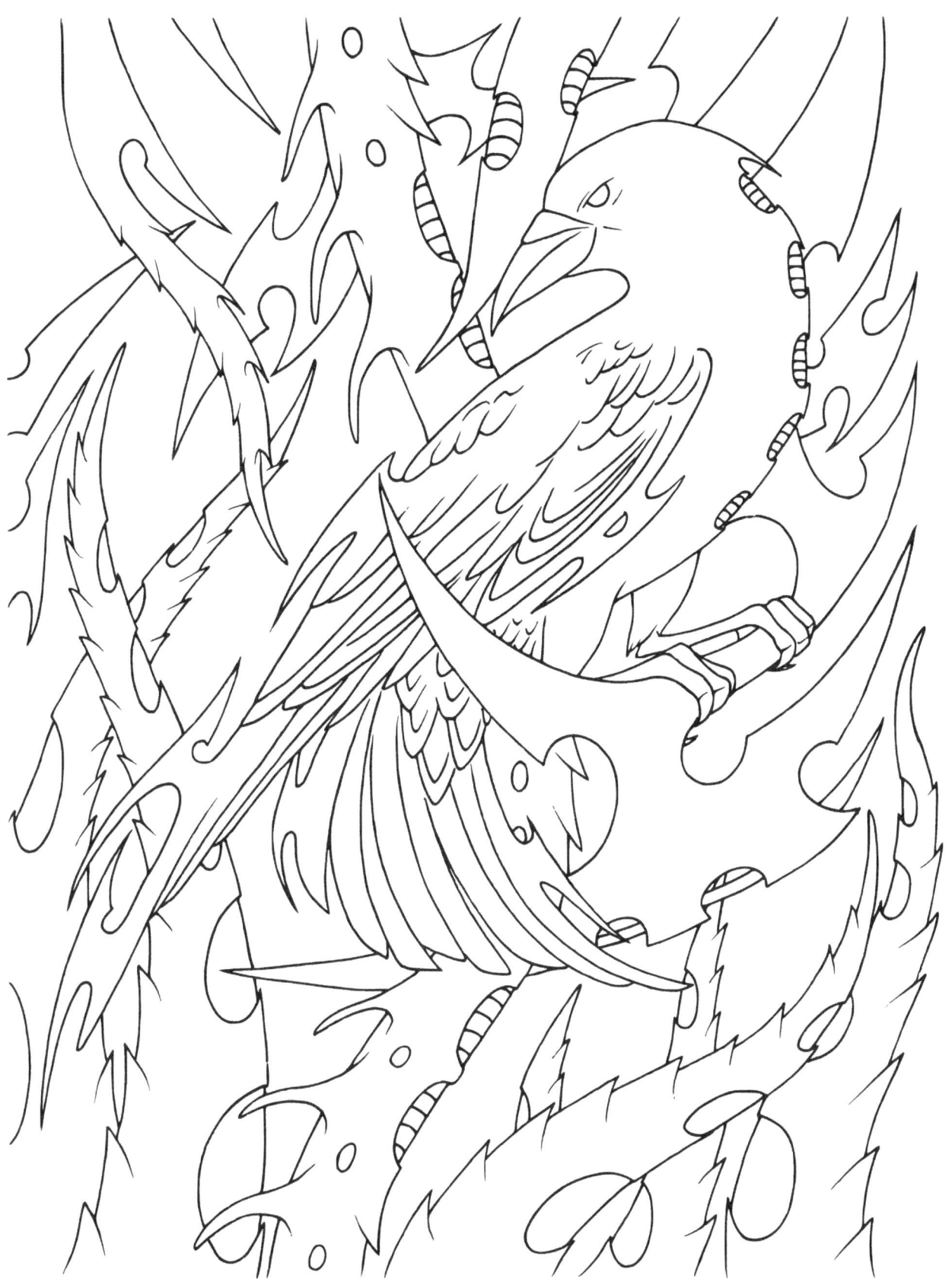

EXTENSITY

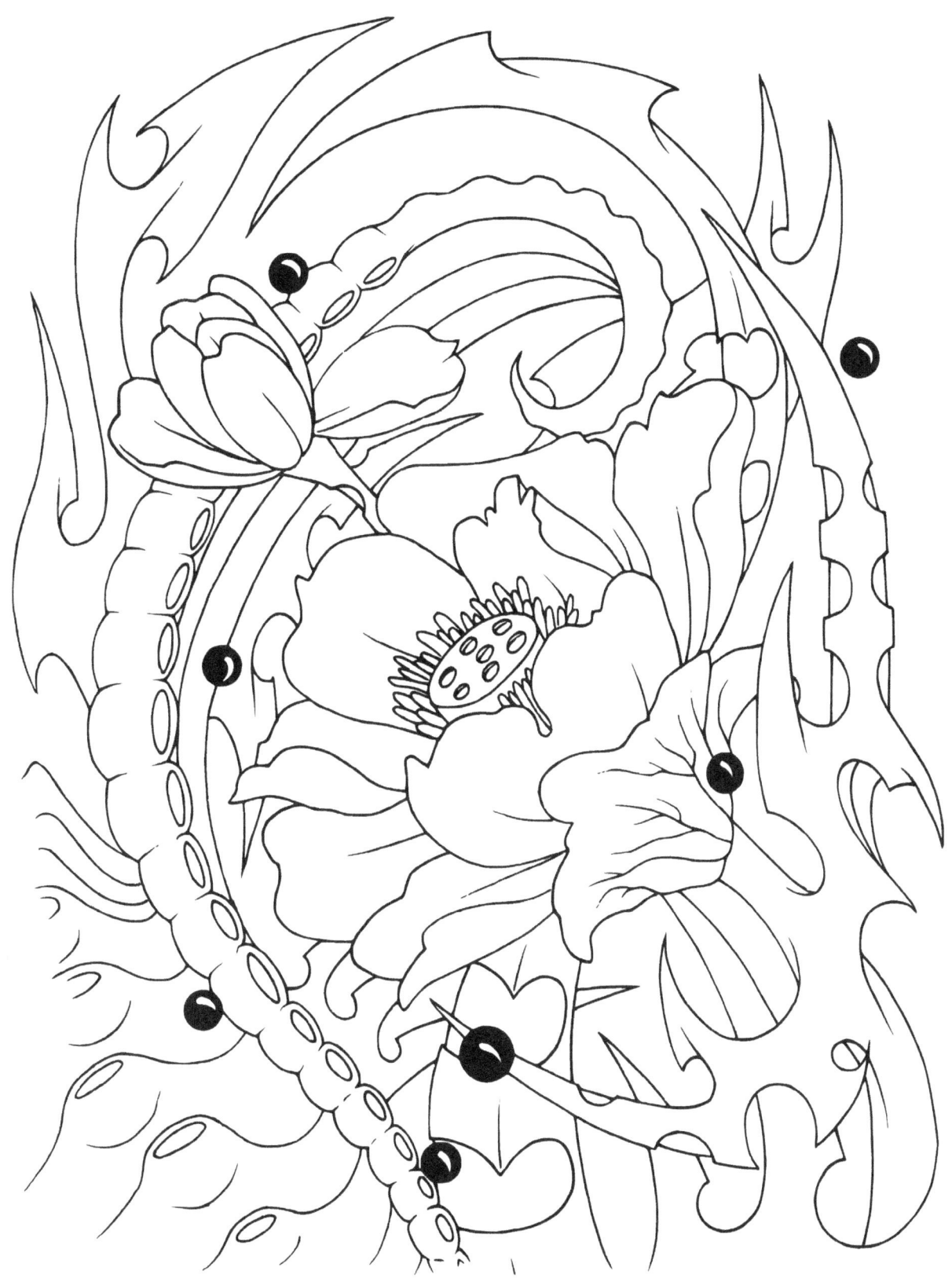

EXTENSITY

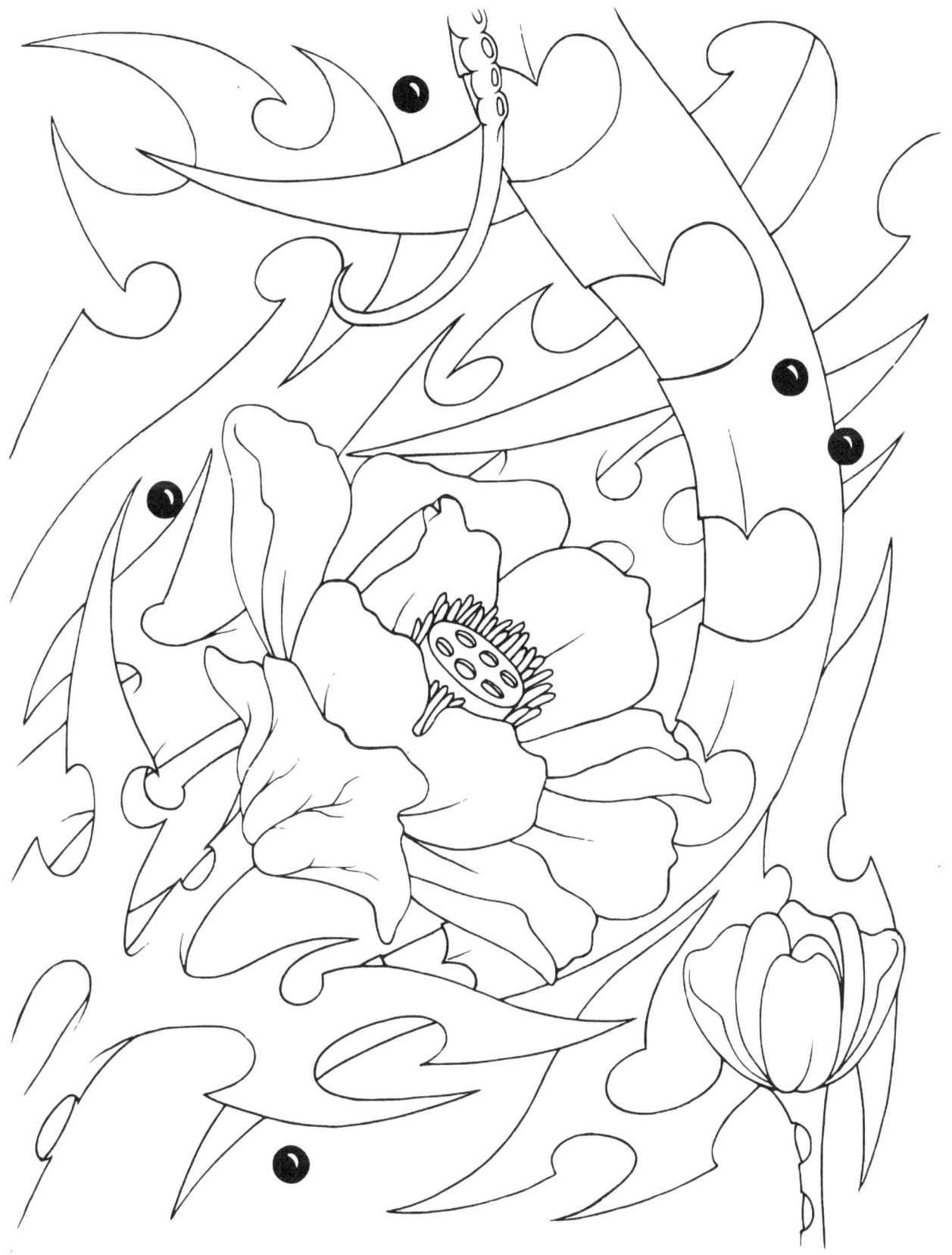

EXTENSITY

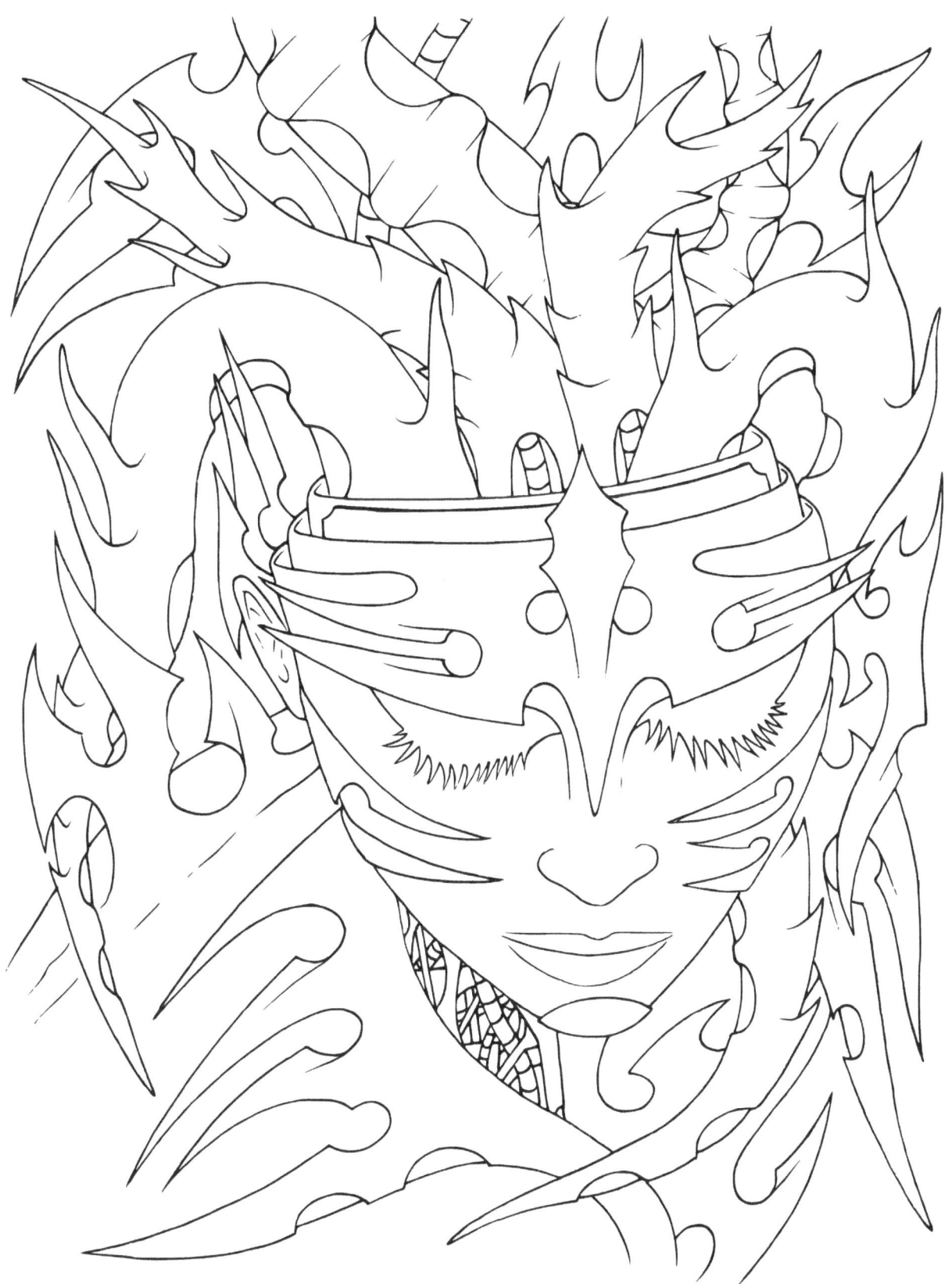

EXTENSITY

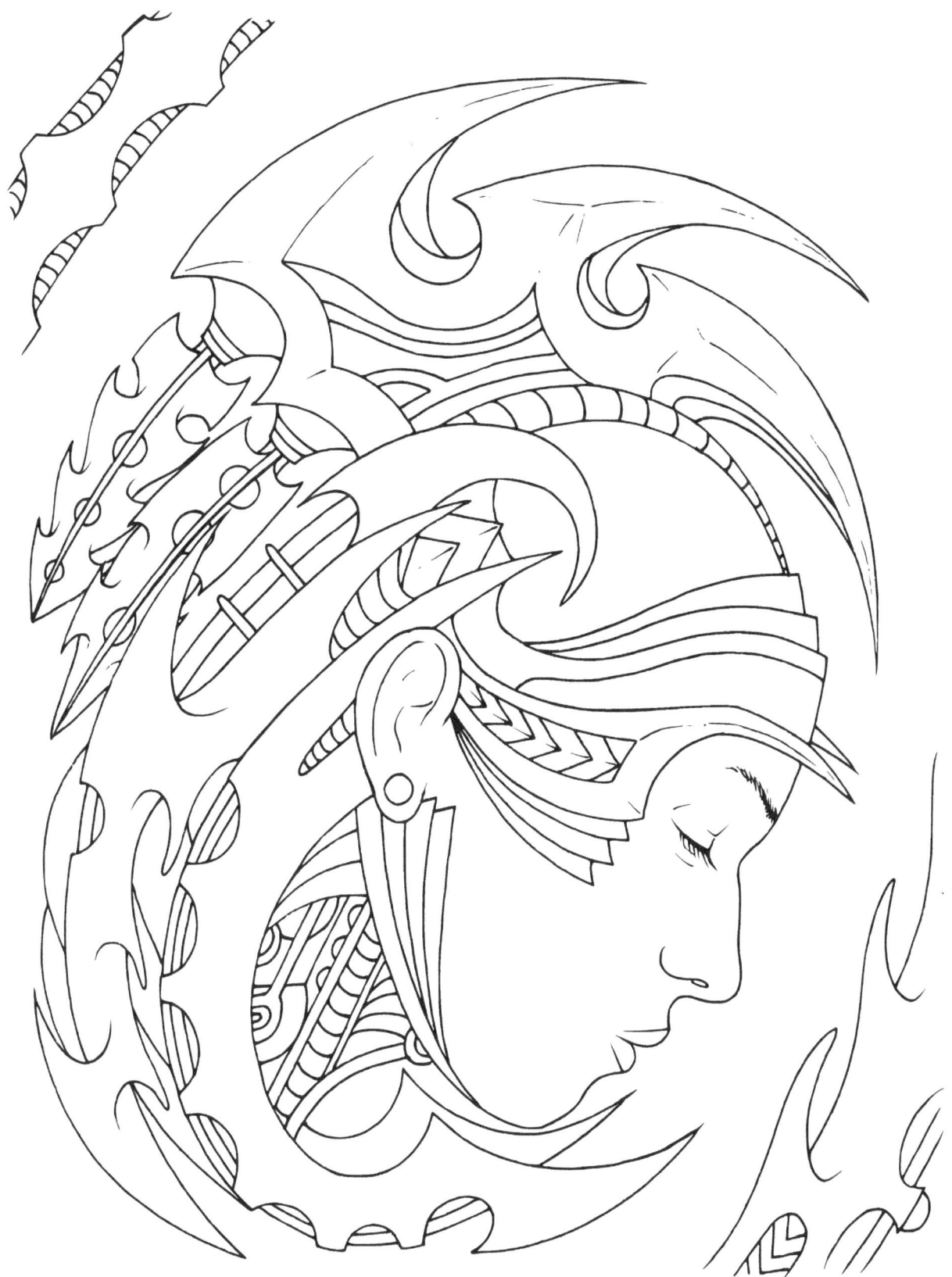

EXTENSITY

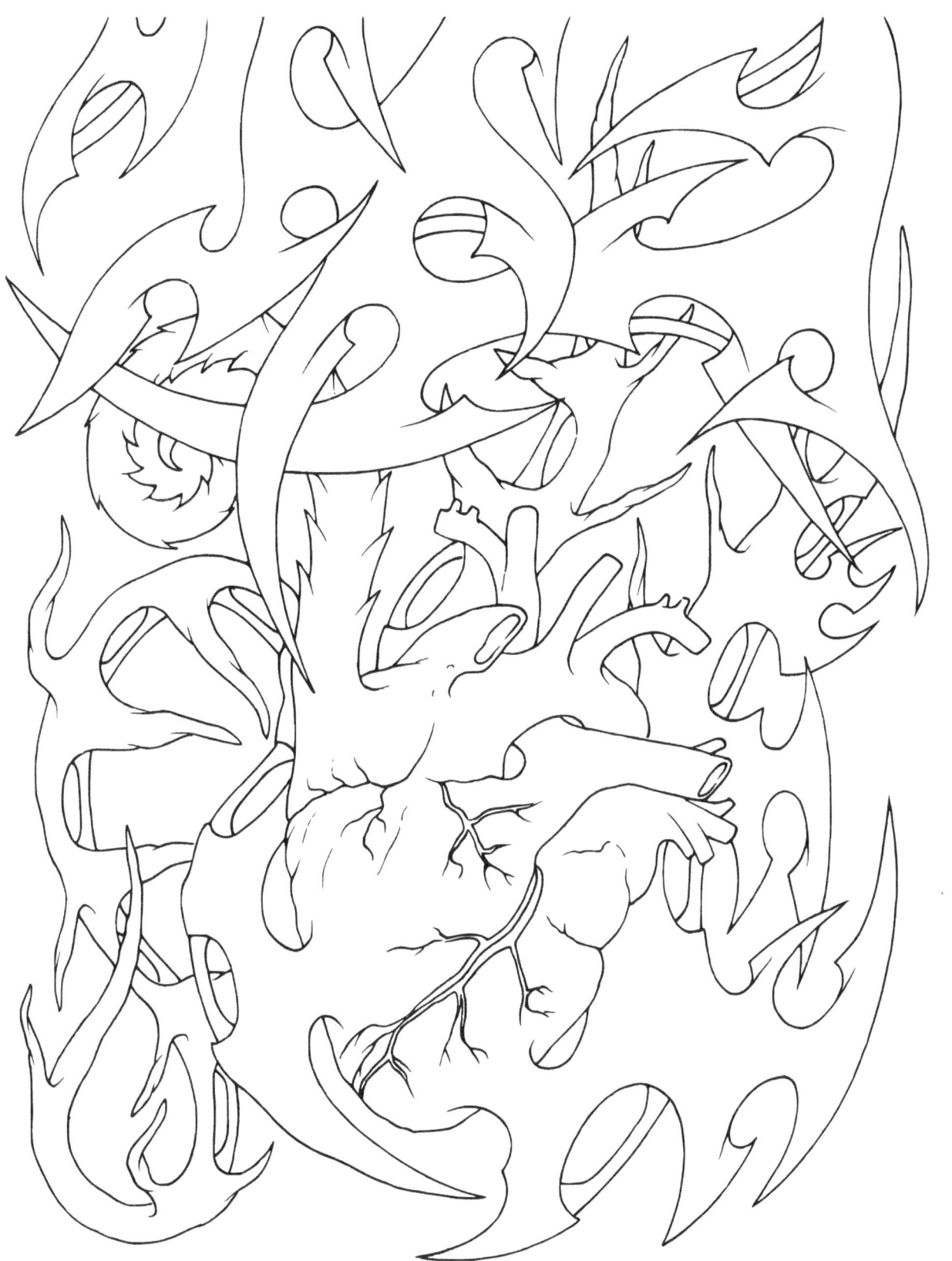

EXTENSITY

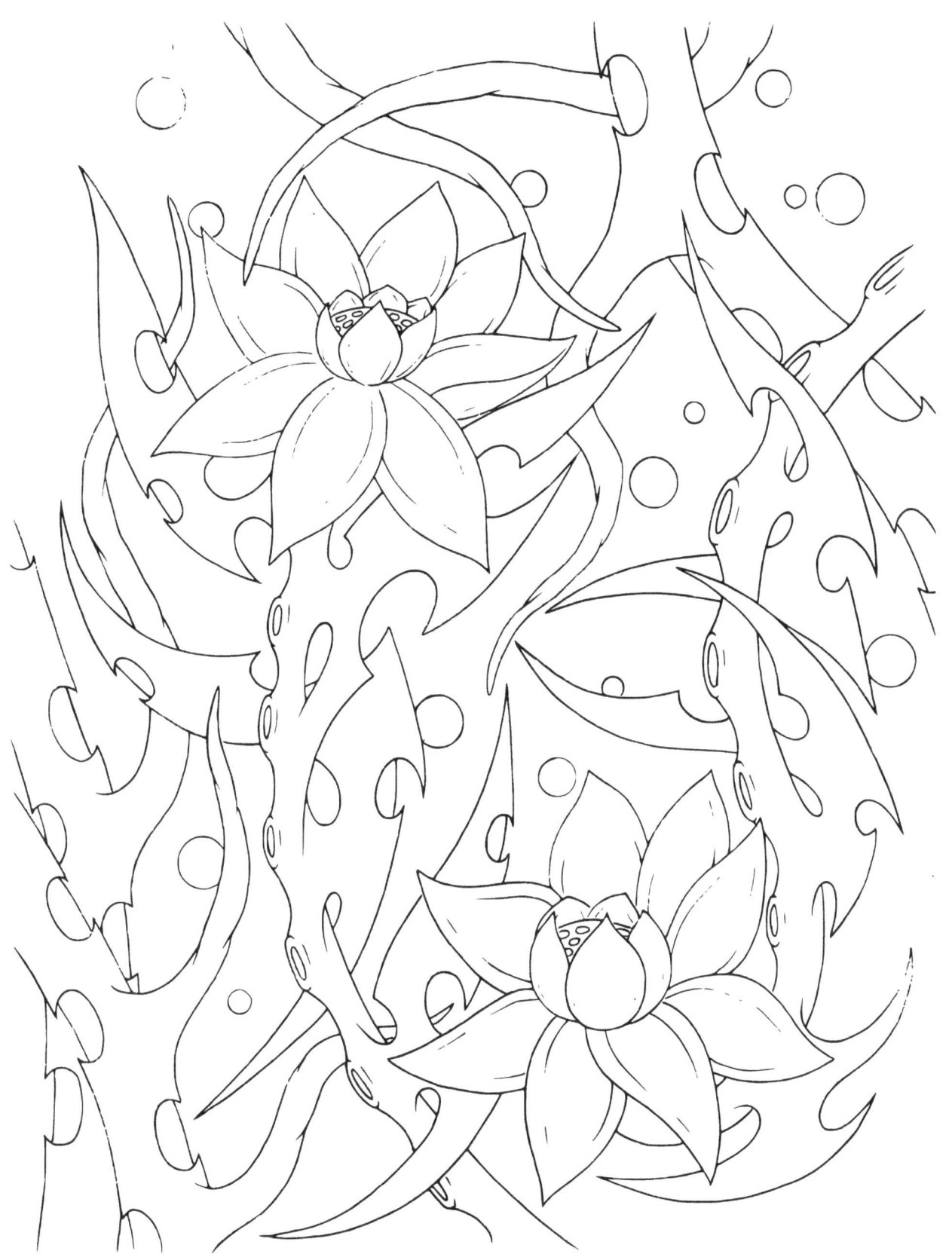

EXTENSITY

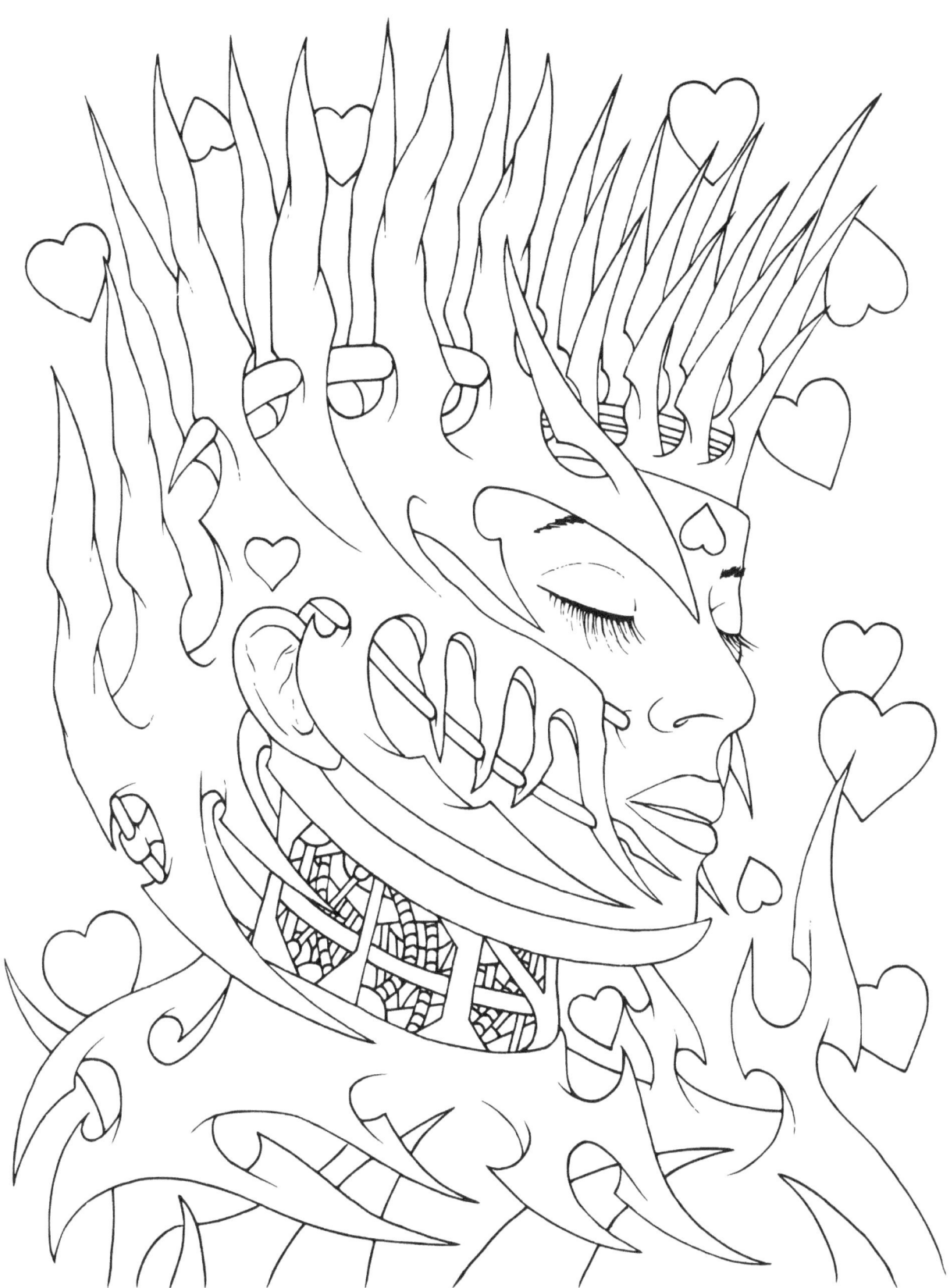

EXTENSITY

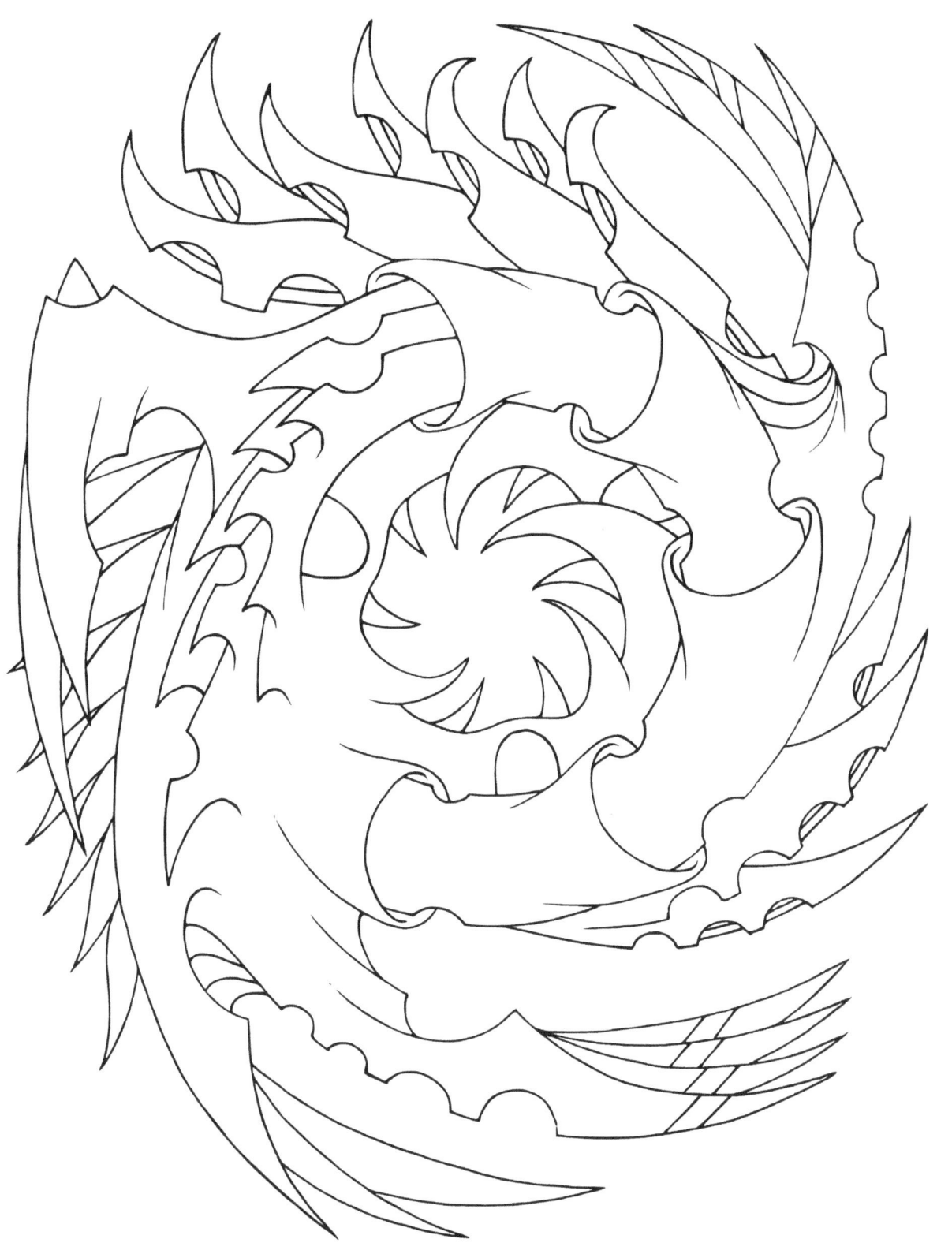

EXTENSITY

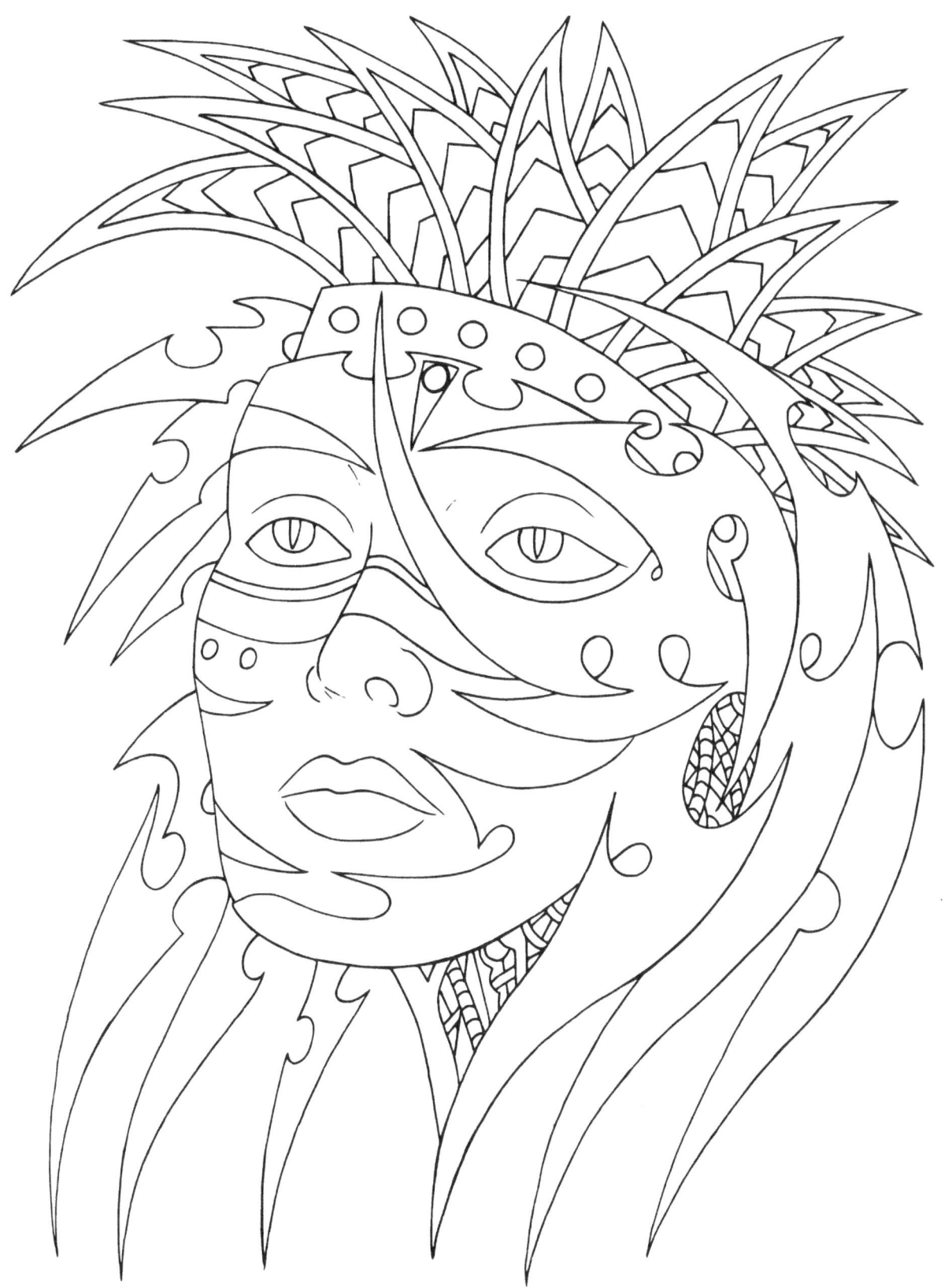

EXTENSITY

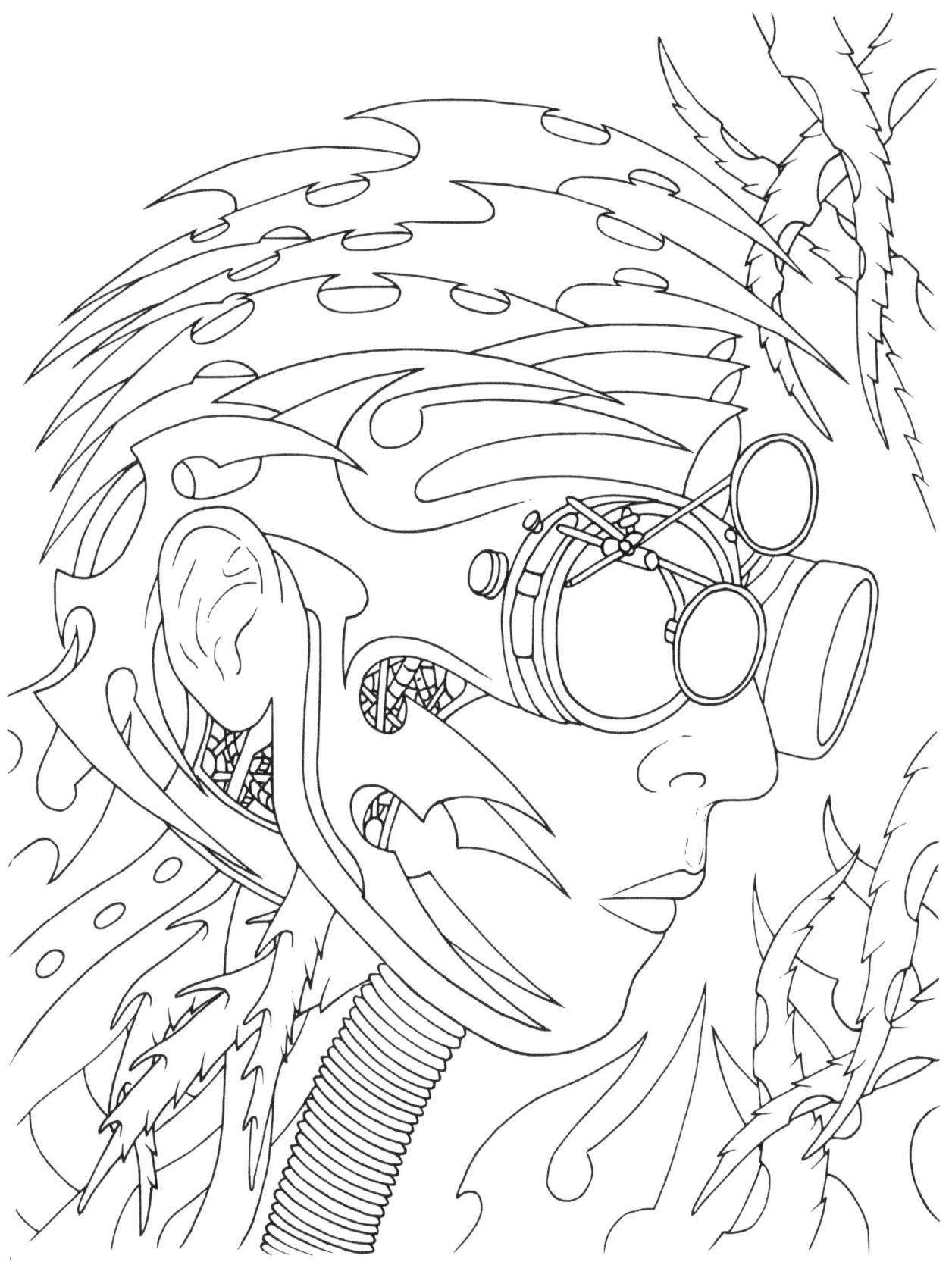

EXTENSITY

THIS COLORING BOOK HAS EXTENSITY PAGES.

THE EXTENSITY PAGES ARE CERTAIN PAGES THAT WHEN PUT

TOGETHER MAKE A LARGER IMAGE. TO FIND WHAT PAGES

WORK TOGETHER LOOK TO THE LEGEND ON THE FOLLOWING

PAGES .

BE SURE TO LOOK OUT FOR EXTENCITY II

COMING IN LATE 2017 FOR MORE EXTENSITY PAGES.

BOOK ONE AND BOOK TWO PUT TOGETHER WILL MAKE

EVEN MORE LARGER IMAGES FOR YOU TO COLOR.

EXTENSITY

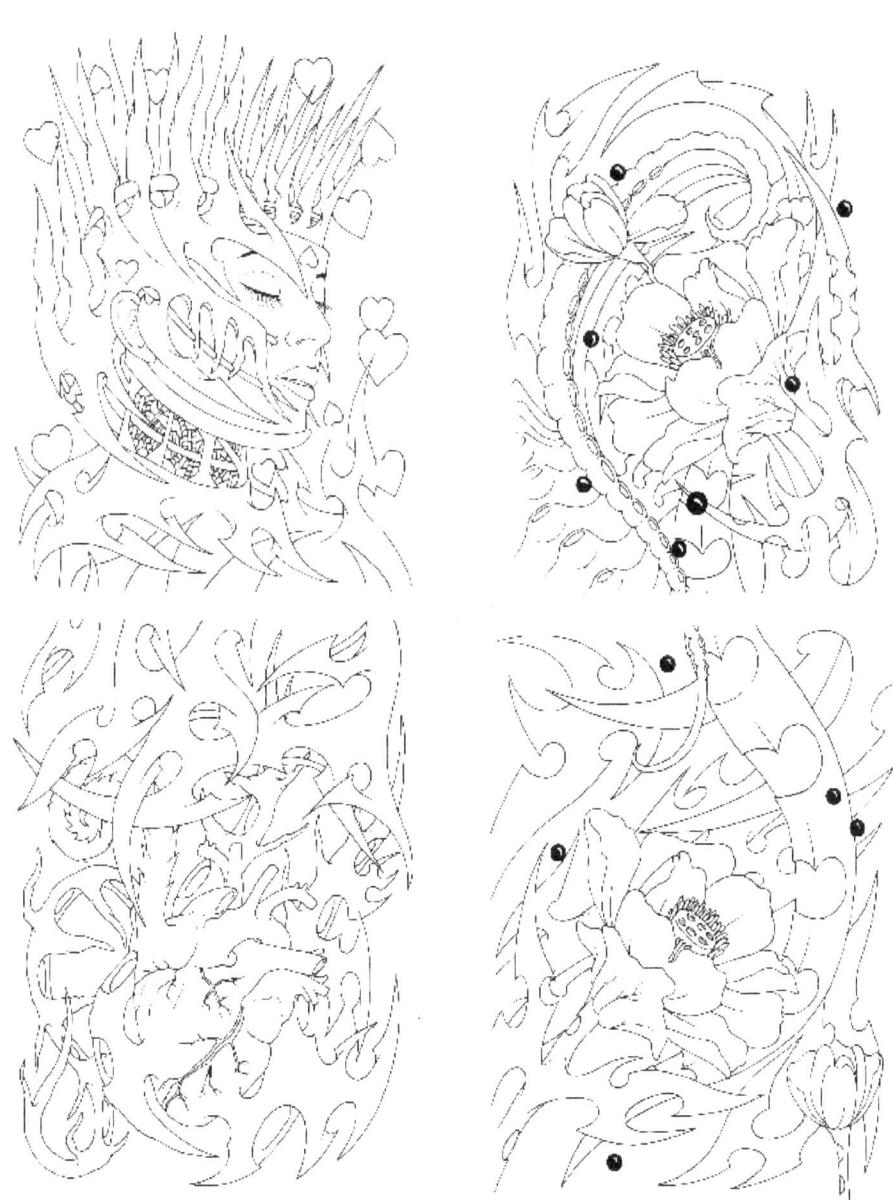

EXTENSITY

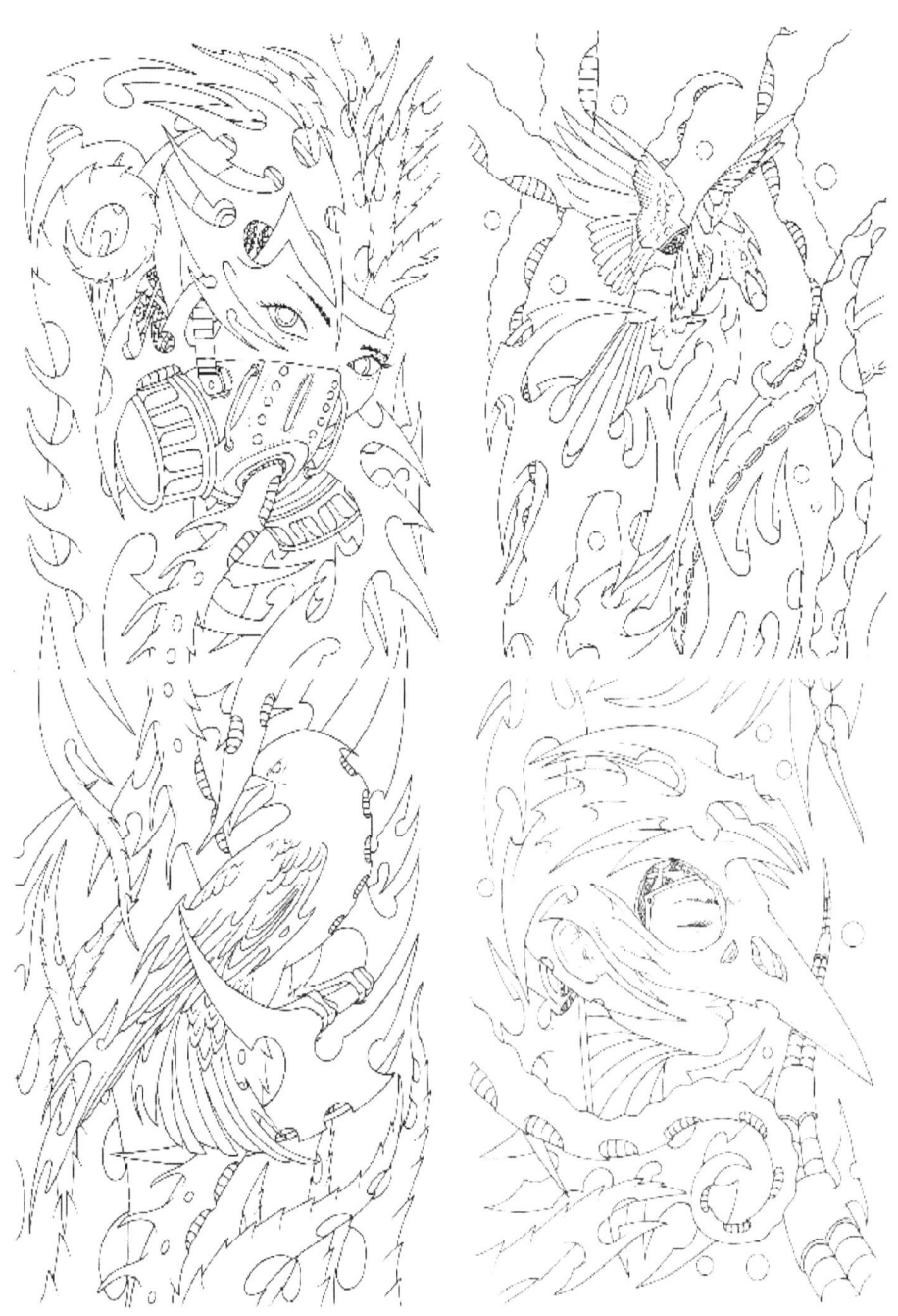

EXTENSITY

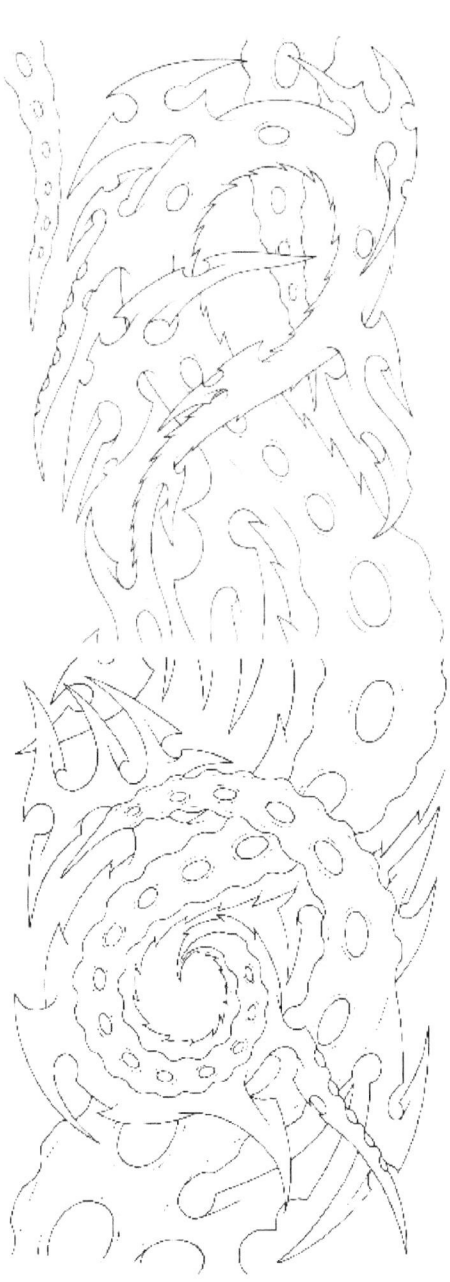

EXTENSITY